ORIGAMI DRESS-UP

MARC KIRSCHENBAUM

FIT TO PRINT PUBLISHING, INC.
NEW YORK, NY

Origami Dress-Up
Copyright © 2022
Fit To Print Publishing, Inc.

All rights reserved. No part of this publication may be reproduced, stored in a retrieval system or transmitted in any form or by any means, electronic, mechanical, photocopying, recording or otherwise, without the permission of the copyright holder.

ISBN 978-1-951146-21-4 (Paperback Edition)
ISBN 978-1-951146-22-1 (Hardcover Edition)

The diagrams in this book were produced with Macromedia's Freehand, and image processing was done with Adobe Photoshop. The Backtalk family of typefaces was used for the body text. Oo Boodlio Doo was used for the cover and the headers. Ellen Cohen assisted with the cover design and provided valuable artistic assistance. Special thanks to Sara Adams for providing some of the papers used.

CONTENTS

Introduction	5
Paper & Materials	6
Symbols & Terminology	8
Plain Face (Long Hair)	12
Plain Face (Short Hair)	17
Detailed Face (Long Hair)	19
Detailed Face (Short Hair)	25
Formalwear	35
Dress	33
Swimsuit	40
Casualwear	48
Face to Body Attachment	58
Angel	60
Cowhand	67
Teddy Bear	78
Witch	88
Sailor	99

INTRODUCTION

Paper dolls have been popular for centuries, likely since the advent of paper. The earliest examples are regarded as some of the first specimens of recorded origami, taking the form of elaborate royal figures in classical garb. Part of the appeal of paper dolls is to mix and match clothing, which is facilitated by the more modern system of gluing tabs of paper to connect doll pieces. This collection of paper dolls matches the custom options of the newer approach with the tradition of origami.

The first selection of dolls consists of four different heads along with four different bodies, where any head can be paired with any of the bodies. The connecting scheme is secure, but easily undone so you can swap out the different sections. Your creativity can also be exercised by exploring different color schemes and there is even some flexibility to try different paper sizes (using the same sized square is recommended for all the pieces if you are unsure).

All the other models in the book are from a single square. A similar look is utilized with the head proportions and stylings as with the multi-piece models. Even the included *Teddy Bear* shares the same folding DNA with the earlier works, especially apparent in how the eyes and nose is formed.

Every effort was made to make these works foldable from readily available origami papers. All of them can be formed from 6" (15cm) squares, but the models with smaller details like eyes will certainly be easier to fold from the larger 10" (25cm) variety of papers.

The models are roughly ordered in increasing level of difficulty, but all of them can be considered intermediate level. Generally, the sequences with more steps might be a little bit more taxing, but not necessarily harder to make. Have fun folding (and playing with) these origami paper dolls!

PAPER & MATERIALS

Picking the perfect paper for your origami project can range from fun to frustrating. There are many origami designs with well over a hundred steps that demand specialty papers that can handle their stressful folding sequences. Fortunately, all these simpler pieces can be made from almost any paper made for origami. While it might be tempting to just use copy paper (or any scrap paper lying around), often such materials are too thick to handle more than a few layers of folds.

One of the better varieties to consider is kami, which is the Japanese word for *paper*. It is often just simply sold as *origami paper*, being extremely common. It can be found on most online stores, hobby shops, and of course origami stores (such as The Source, which is part of OrigamiUSA). The standard size is six inches (or fifteen centimeters) which is suitable for these projects. You could also consider the larger ten-inch size (or twenty-five-centimeter variety).

Most kami papers sport a decorative side (either plain or patterned) with the other side being plain white. A few of the models showcase both sides of the paper, so you should consider the *duo* or *double-sided* variety of kami. Of course, stay clear from the papers that are simply the same color on both sides.

Other papers sold for origami purposes are not as easy to work with. Foil backed papers do look nice and shiny when they are pristine, but they will pick up any extraneous creases as you fold. Some sequences call for changing a valley fold to a mountain fold, and foil papers a notoriously inflexible at that task. Washi papers are typically very durable, but do not often hold a crease well without special treatment. One solution is to use glue while folding, with PVA adhesives being ideal.

More adventurous folders might consider custom paper preparations. This can be as simple as using a favorite giftwrap and cutting it down to size. If you are considering getting a paper cutter, rotary style is more accurate and far safer than the guillotine kind. A popular European wrapping paper variety is known as *kraft* paper, which is the German word for *strong*. Most origami shops will sell it precut into squares. Like most wrapping paper, it is plain on the other side. Some origami artists will paint their papers with watered down acrylic paints. Many of the models showcased here were prepared with these papers, with the plain side representing the skin tones.

If you do wish to color the other side of your paper, a less messy approach is to glue a lightweight sheet onto the other side. A perfect adhesive for this application is methylcellulose, often abbreviated as *MC*. MC comes in a powder form that needs to be mixed into cold water. About two teaspoons per 1.5 cups of water is a good ratio. After about thirty minutes of periodic stirring the MC will reach a syrupy consistency. It can be brushed on your paper (any cheap paintbrush is fine) after which you can place your thinner paper atop. You can then brush more MC for a better bond. The drying process can be accelerated with a table fan. Many of the models showcased here were prepared with this technique. Have fun experimenting with different materials.

SYMBOLS & TERMINOLOGY

Valley Fold

A dashed line with an open-headed arrow indicates to *Valley Fold* (fold forward in the direction of the arrow).

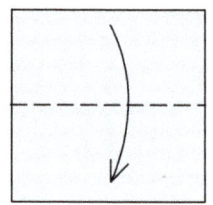 

1. Valley fold in half.   2. Completed *Valley Fold*.

Mountain Fold

A dashed line with dots along with a closed-headed arrow indicates to *Mountain Fold* (fold behind in the direction of the arrow).

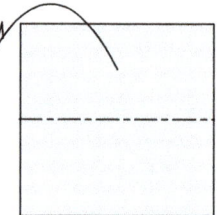 

1. Mountain fold in half.   2. Completed *Mountain Fold*.

Precrease

A valley fold line with a double-headed arrow indicates to Precrease (valley fold and then unfold in the direction of the open headed arrow). The resulting *crease* is represented by a thin line.

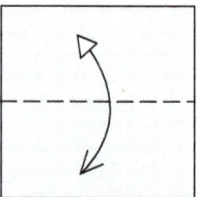 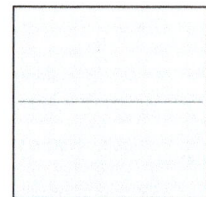

1. Precrease in half.   2. Completed *Precrease*.

Turn Over

Turn over is indicated by a looped arrow.

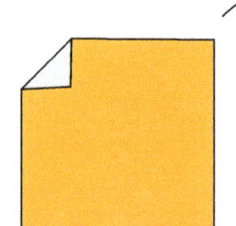 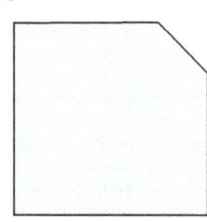

Rotate

Rotate is indicated by a circle with arrows along it.

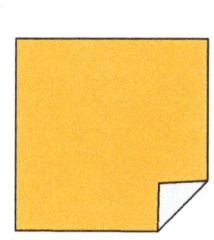

Hidden / Imaginary Lines

Hidden/Imaginary lines are indicated by a thin dotted line.

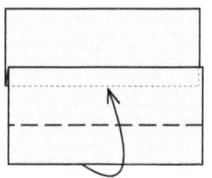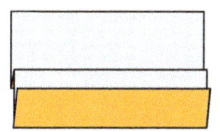

1. Valley fold to the hidden edge.
2. Completed fold.

Angle Bisectors

Open dots are sometimes used to indicate angle bisectors.

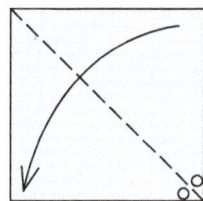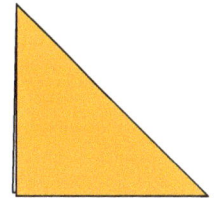

1. Valley fold along the indicated angle bisector.
2. Completed fold.

Divided Brackets

A divided bracket with tick marks shows equal divisions.

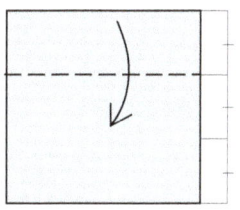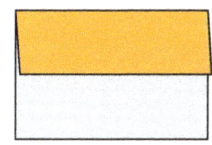

1. Valley fold along the 1/3rd mark.
2. Completed *Valley Fold*.

Reference Dots

Dots are sometimes used to call attention to a specific landmark.

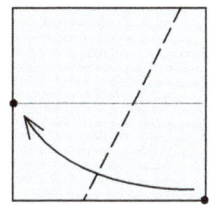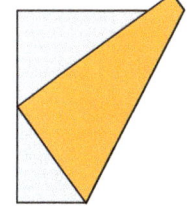

1. Valley fold the dotted corner to the dotted crease.
2. Completed fold.

Pleat Fold

A *Pleat Fold* is indicated by a mountain fold line followed by a valley fold line. An arrow indicates the direction of the pleat.

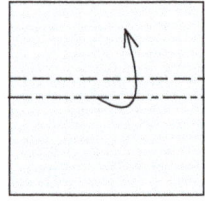 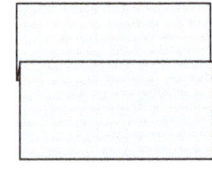

1. Pleat fold upwards.   2. Completed *Pleat Fold*.

Reverse Fold

A solid arrow indicates to push in or invert at the indicated area for a *Reverse Fold*, *Squash Fold* or various types of *Sink Folds*. For a *Reverse Fold*, you invert the indicated section.

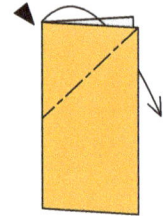 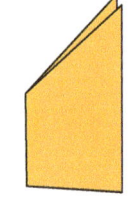

1. Reverse fold the corner.   2. Completed *Reverse Fold*.

Squash Fold

A *Squash Fold* is a combination of a reverse fold with opening out the inverted area.

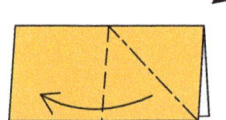 

1. Squash fold the corner.   2. Completed *Squash Fold*.

Sink Fold

A *Sink Fold* is related to a reverse fold, but it is performed on a point from the middle of the paper. After precreasing where this fold occurs, you open out the point and invert it along the perimeter of the creases.

1. Sink fold the corner.   2. Completed *Sink Fold*.

Petal Fold

A *Petal Fold* is indicated by an open headed arrow with squash fold arrows. A layer is raised up, causing side edges to get pulled inwards and squash folded flat.

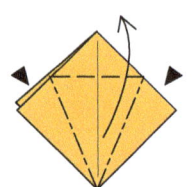 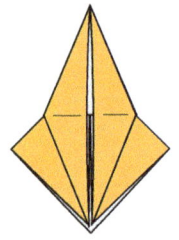

1. Petal fold the corner.   2. Completed *Petal Fold*.

Petal Fold

A *Petal Fold* is indicated by an open headed arrow with squash fold arrows. A layer is raised up, causing side edges to get pulled inwards and squash folded flat.

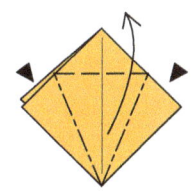
1. Petal fold the corner.

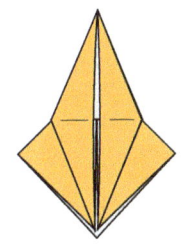
2. Completed *Petal Fold*.

Outside Reverse Fold

An *Outside Reverse Fold* is indicated by a set of arrows. You wrap around the indicated layer and flatten.

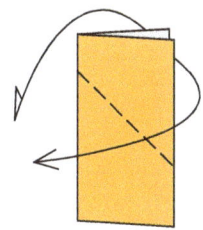
1. Outside reverse fold the corner.

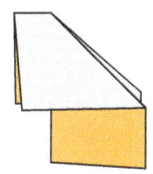
2. Completed *Outside Reverse Fold*.

Spread Squash

A *Spread Squash* is a sink fold that is spread open.

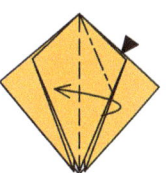
1. Spread squash the corner.

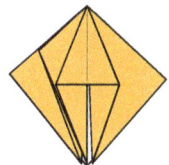
2. Completed *Spread Squash*.

Swivel Fold

Swivel Fold is indicated by a set of arrows and sometimes accompanied with a sink arrow. Edges are folded over in two different areas, while the connecting paper is squash folded flat.

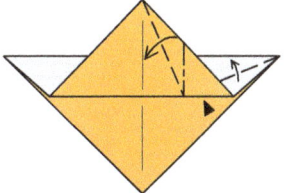
1. Swivel fold the corner.

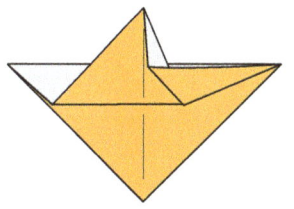
2. Completed *Swivel Fold*.

Rabbit Ear

Rabbit Ear is indicated by a set of arrows. Two edges are valley folded in, while the connecting paper is pinched flat into a new flap.

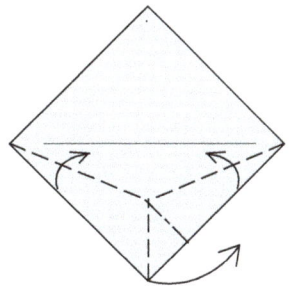
1. Rabbit ear the corner.

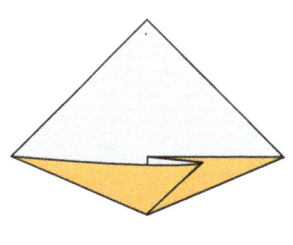
2. Completed *Rabbit Ear*.

PLAIN FACE (LONG HAIR)

plain face (long hair)

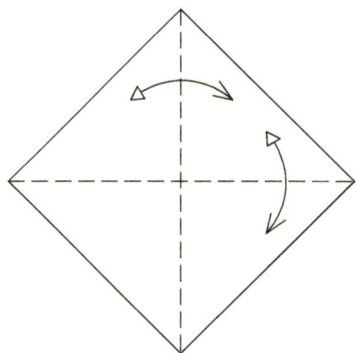

1. Precrease along the diagonals.

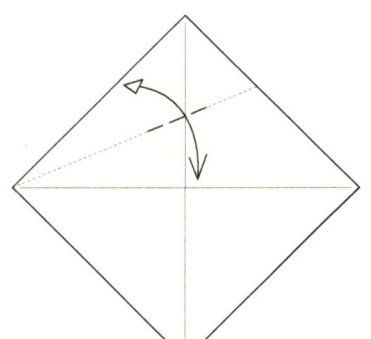

2. Precrease along the angle bisector, only creasing at the middle.

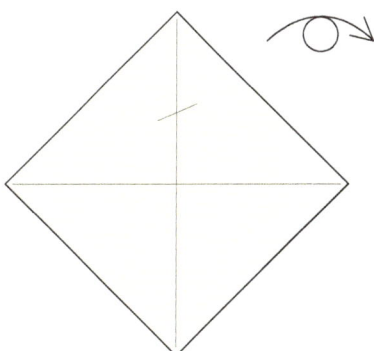

3. Turn over.

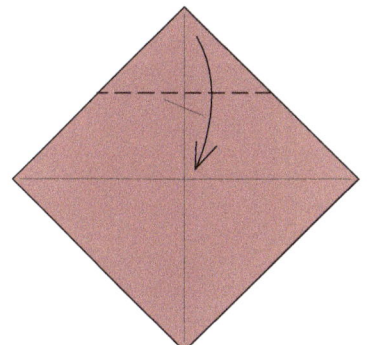

4. Valley fold to the center.

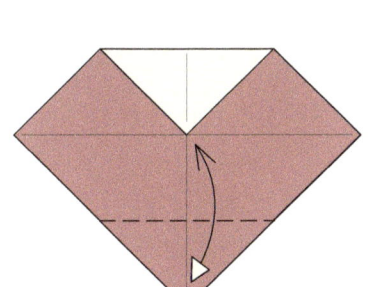

5. Precrease to the center.

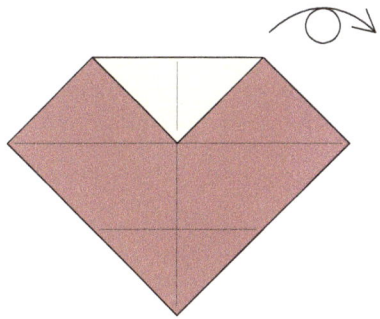

6. Turn over.

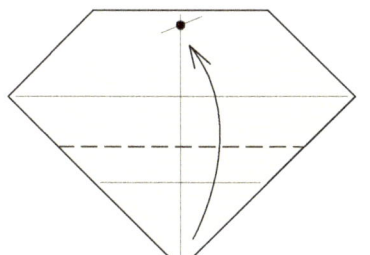

7. Valley fold to the dotted intersection of creases.

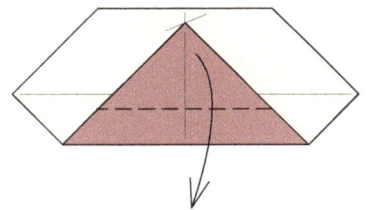

8. Valley fold along the existing crease.

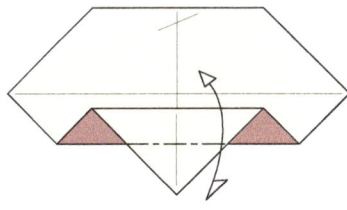

9. Precrease with a mountain fold, aligning with the hidden edge.

13

plain face (long hair)

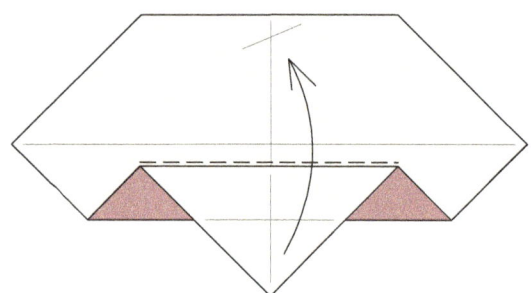

10. Swing the top flap up.

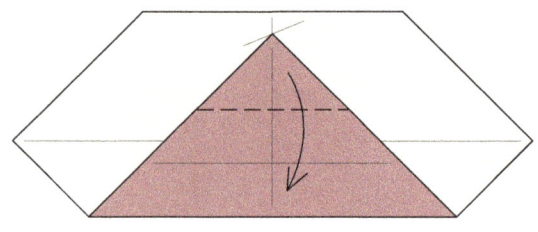

11. Valley fold down along the existing crease.

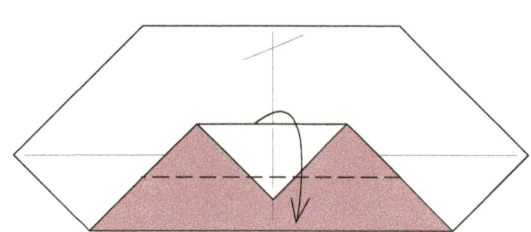

12. Valley fold through both layers long the existing crease.

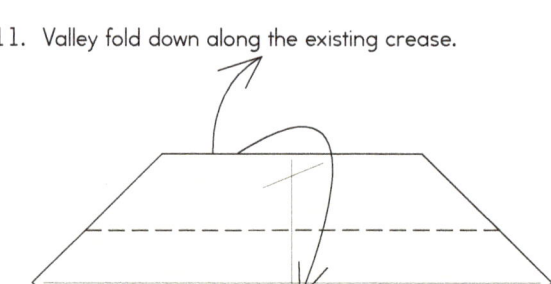

13. Valley fold to the folded edge, allowing the flap from behind to flip forward.

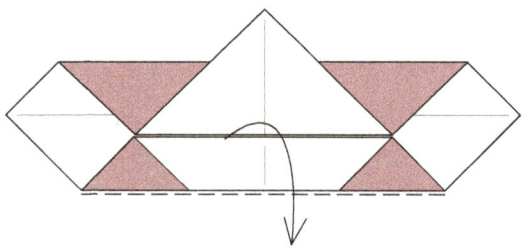

14. Swing down the bottom edge.

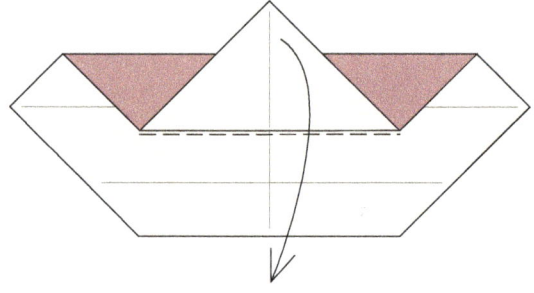

15. Swing down the top flap.

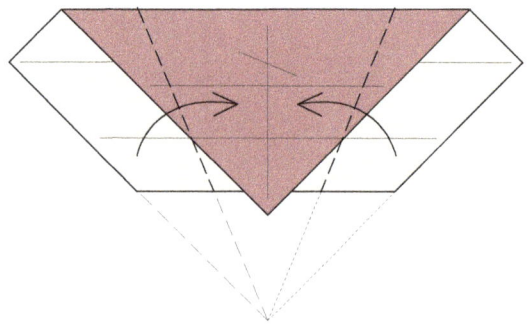

16. Valley fold the sides to the center.

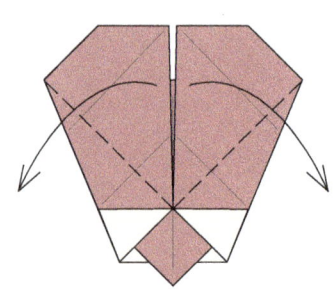

17. Valley fold the top layers outwards.

plain face (long hair)

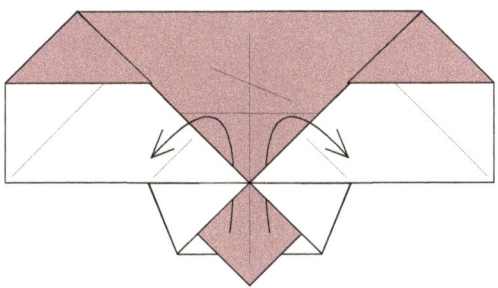

18. Pull out the trapped single layers at each side.

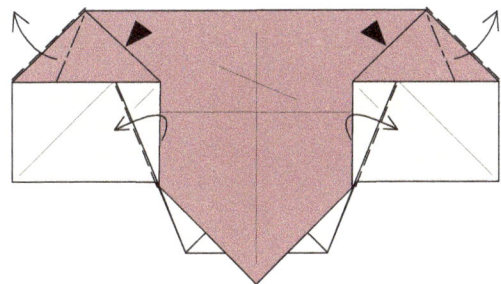

19. Swivel fold the sides upwards.

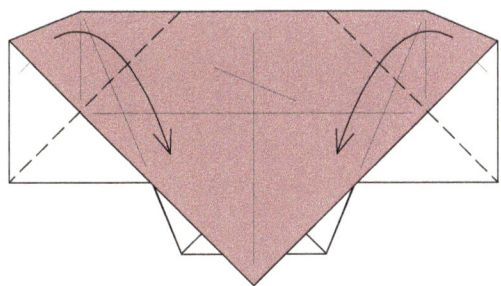

20. Valley fold the sides in half.

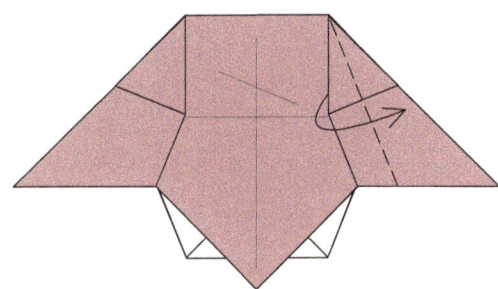

21. Valley fold along the angle bisector.

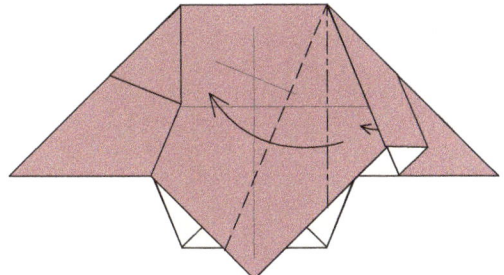

22. Squash fold while pulling out the trapped single layer.

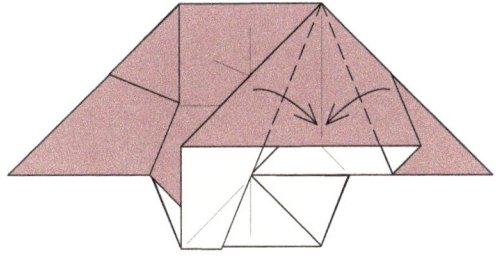

23. Valley fold the sides to the center.

plain face (long hair)

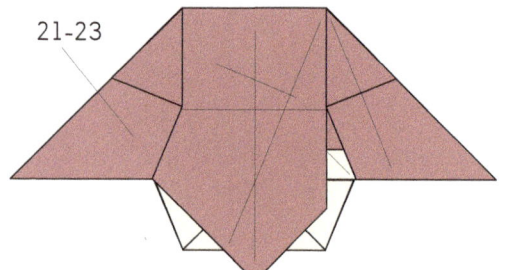

24. Repeat steps 21-23 in mirror image.

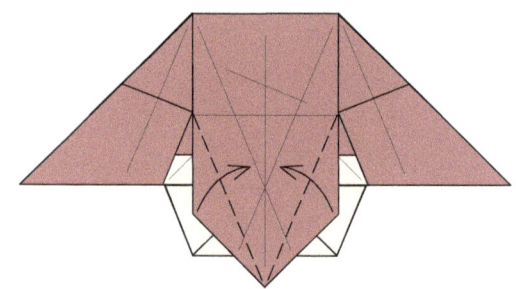

25. Valley fold the sides to the center.

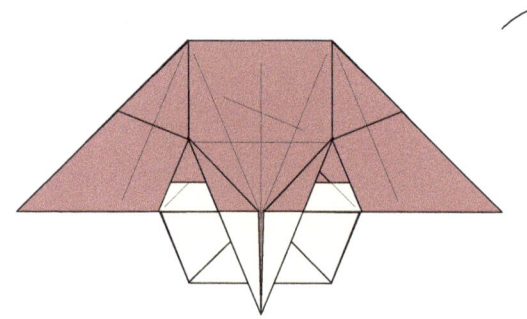

26. Turn over.

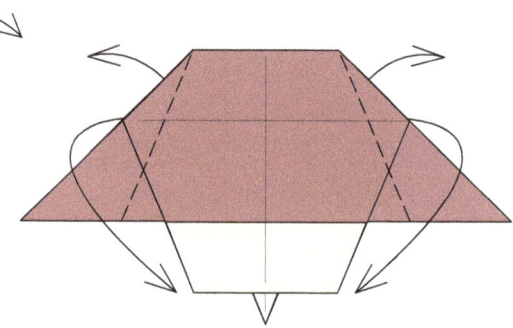

27. Valley fold the sides, allowing the flaps from behind to flip forward.

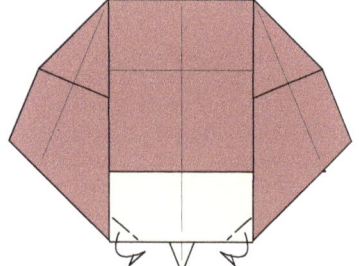

28. Mountain fold the corners.

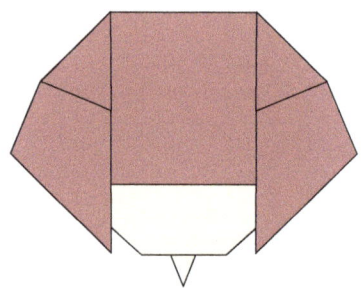

29. Completed *Plain Face (Long Hair)*.

PLAIN FACE (SHORT HAIR)

plain face (short hair)

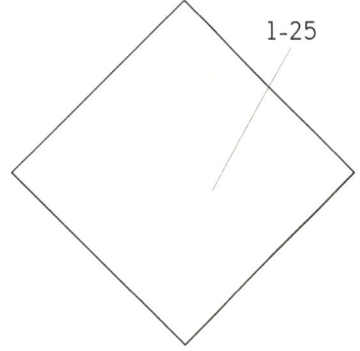

1. Fold steps 1-25 of *Plain Face (Long Hair)*.

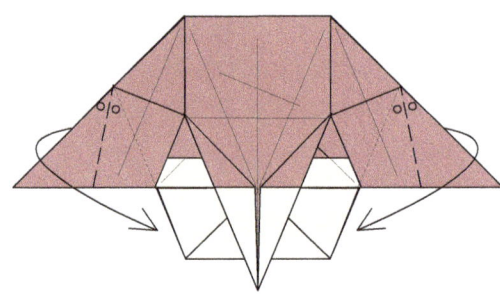

2. Valley fold the sides along the indicated angle bisectors.

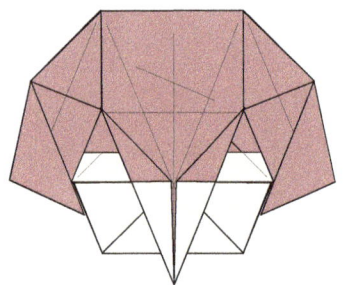

3. Turn over.

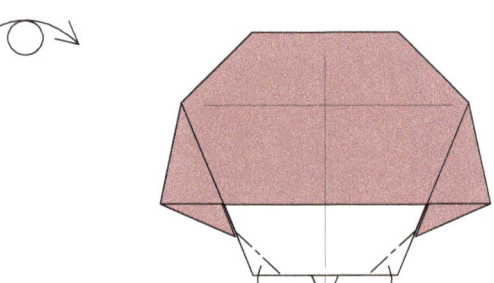

4. Mountain fold the corners.

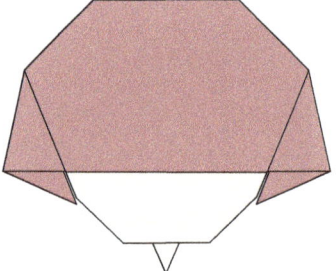

5. Completed *Plain Face (Short Hair)*.

DETAILED FACE (LONG HAIR)

detailed face (long hair)

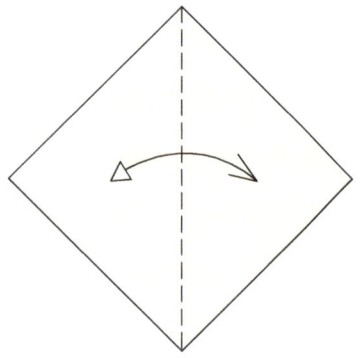

1. Precrease along the diagonal.

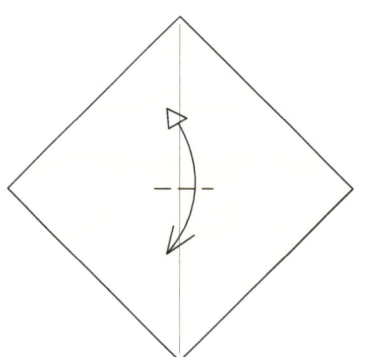

2. Precrease the middle in half.

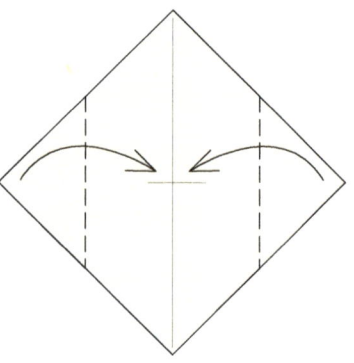

3. Valley fold the sides to the center.

4. Turn over.

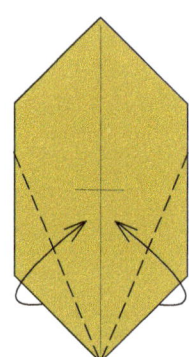

5. Valley fold the bottom edges to the center.

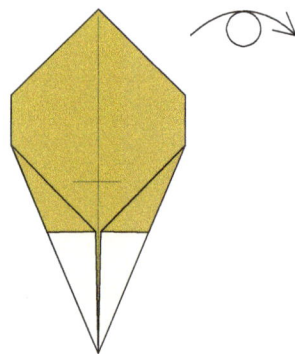

6. Turn over.

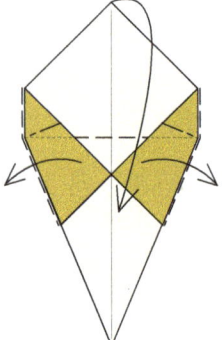

7. Open out the sides, allowing the top to squash fold down.

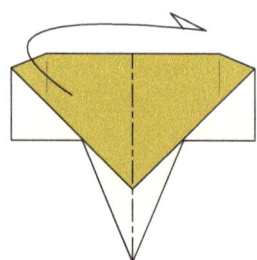

8. Mountain fold in half.

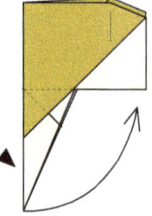

9. Reverse fold the flap up to lie along the edge.

detailed face (long hair)

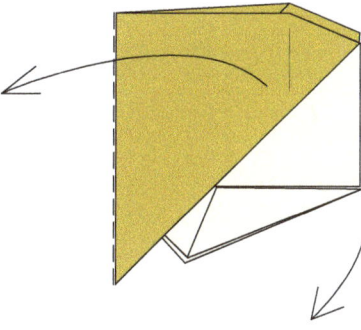

10. Open out along the center, undoing the last reverse fold.

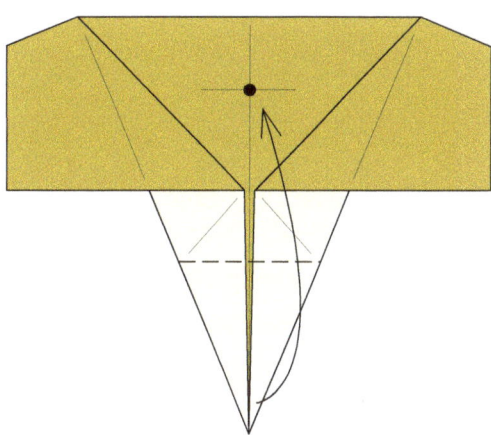

11. Valley fold to the dotted intersection of creases.

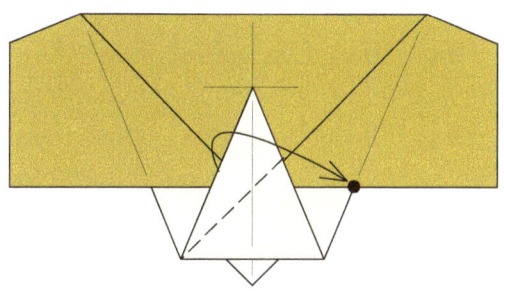

12. Valley fold the flap to the dotted corner.

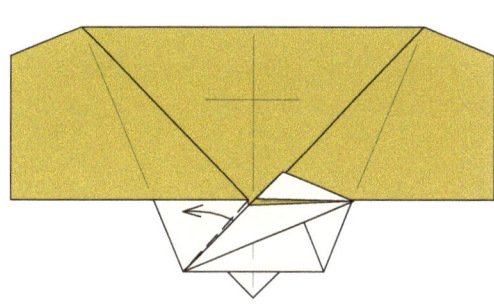

13. Pull out the trapped corner.

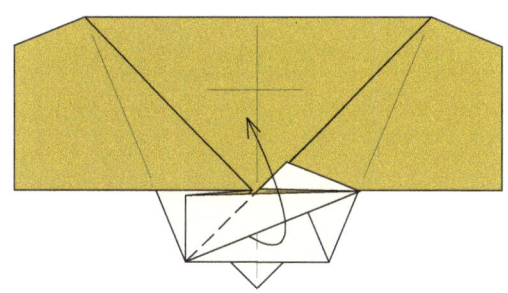

14. Swing the flap back up.

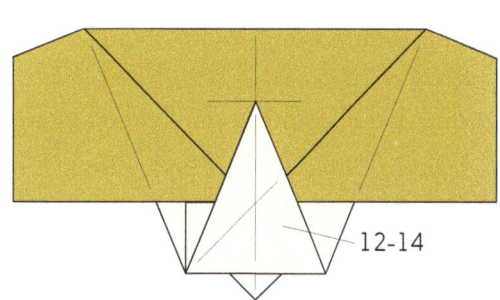

15. Repeat steps 12-14 in mirror image.

detailed face (long hair)

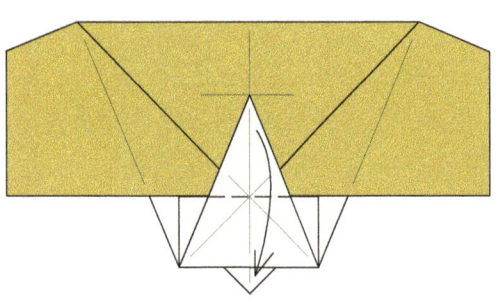

16. Valley fold the flap down.

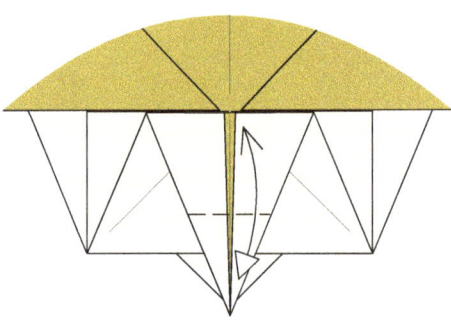

17. Precrease the top flap in half.

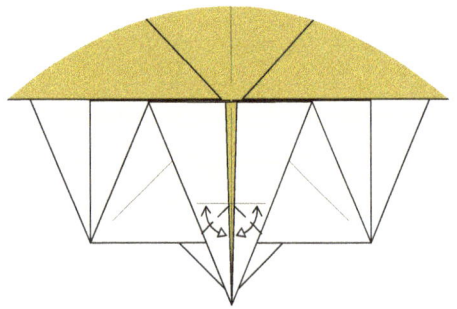

18. Precrease the flap along the angle bisectors.

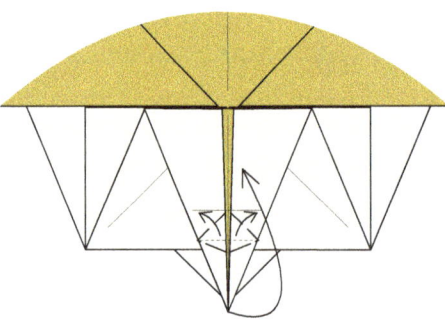

19. Open out the top layers, squash folding the flap up.

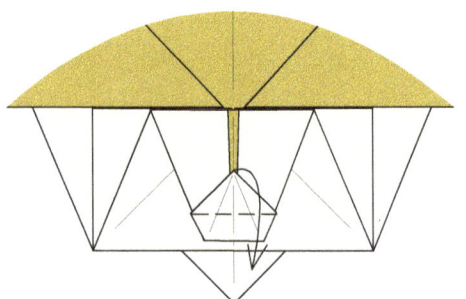

20. Valley fold the corner down.

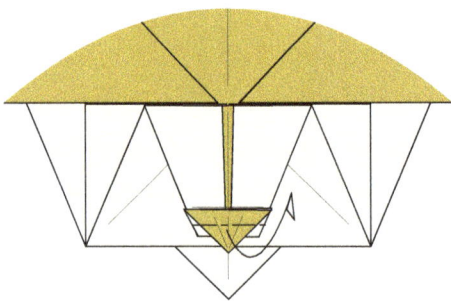

21. Mountain fold the double layer.

detailed face (long hair)

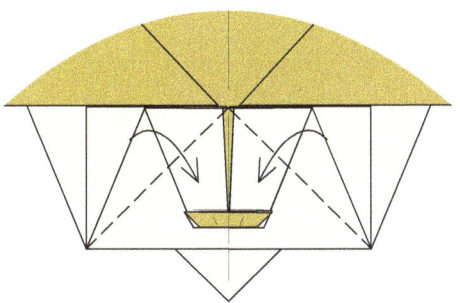

22. Valley fold the flaps inwards.

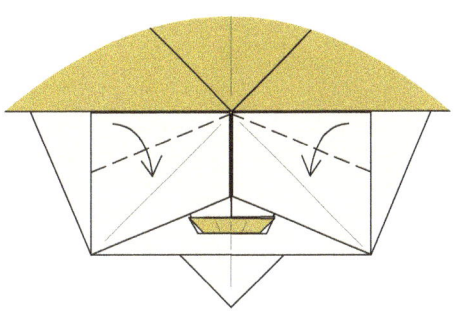

23. Valley fold the flaps to the creases.

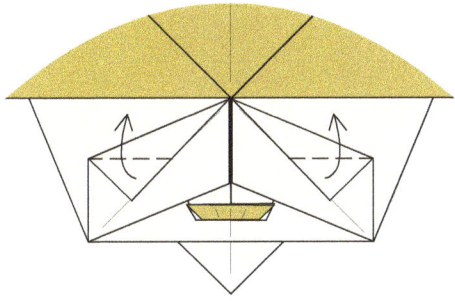

24. Valley fold the corners up.

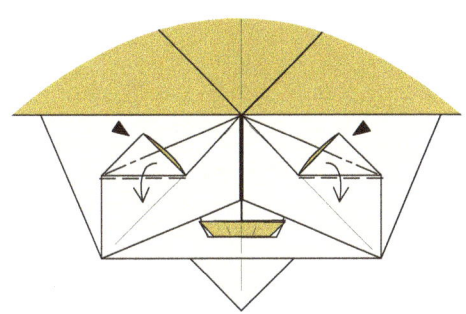

25. Squash fold the flaps.

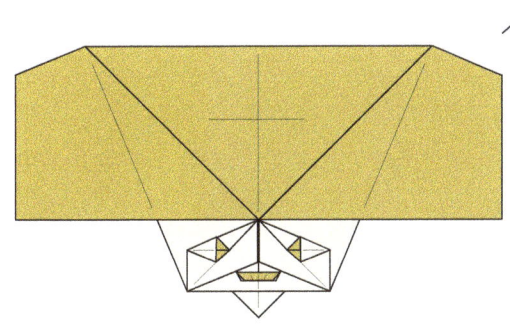

26. Turn over.

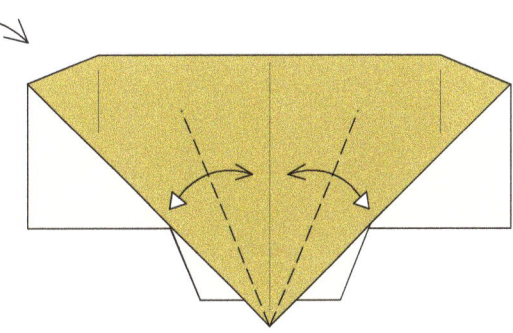

27. Precrease part of the top layer.

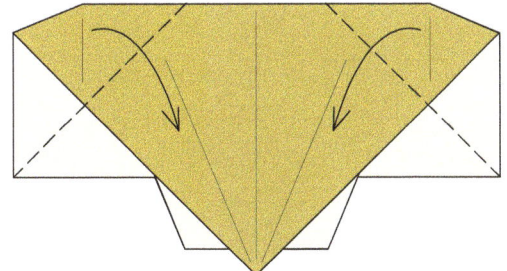

28. Valley fold the corners in half.

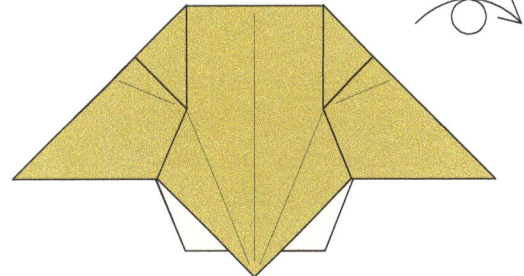

29. Turn over.

detailed face (long hair)

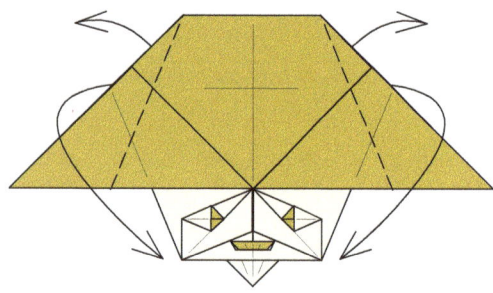

30. Valley fold the sides so they lie straight, allowing the flaps from behind to flip outwards.

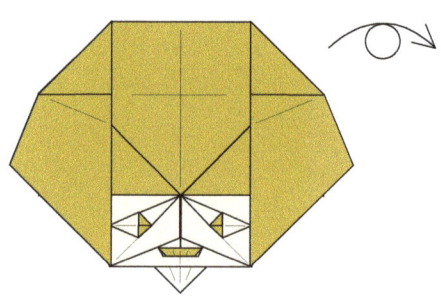

31. Turn over.

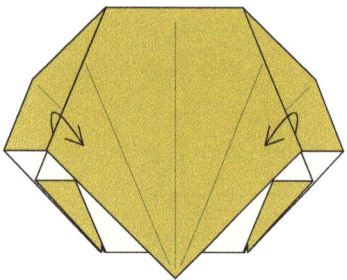

32. Unwrap the top single layer from within the pleated sections.

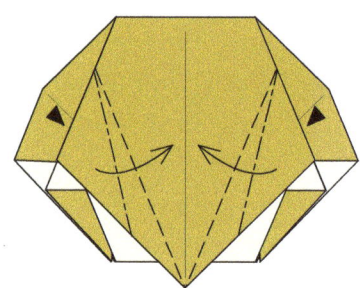

33. Valley fold the sides in to the center, squash folding at the top.

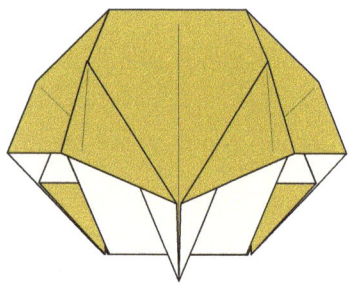

34. Turn over.

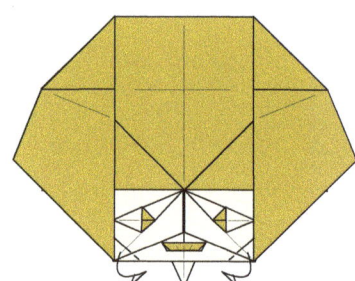

35. Mountain fold the corners.

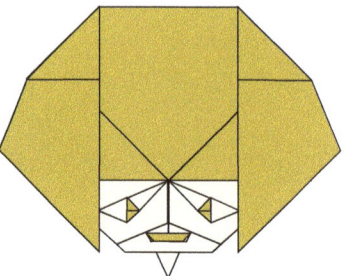

36. Completed *Detailed Face (Long Hair)*.

DETAILED FACE (SHORT HAIR)

detailed face (short hair)

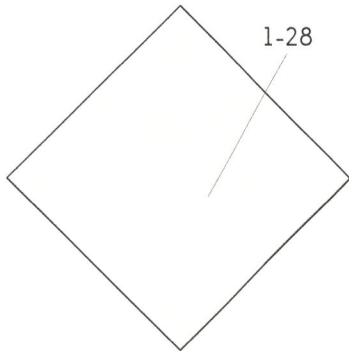

1. Fold steps 1-28 of *Detailed Face (Long Hair)*.

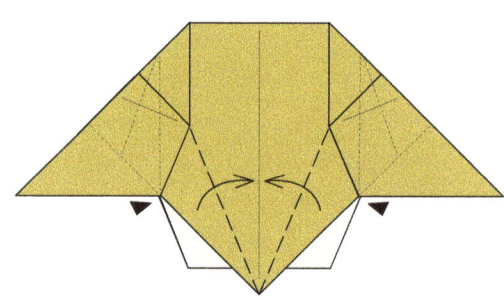

2. Valley fold the sides in, forming hidden swivel folds.

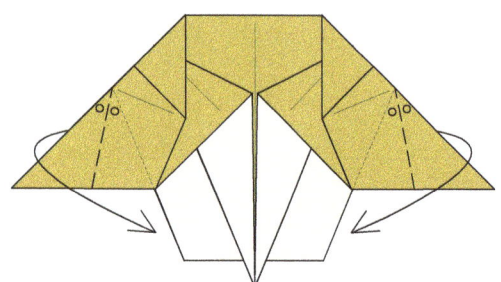

3. Valley fold along the indicated angle bisectors.

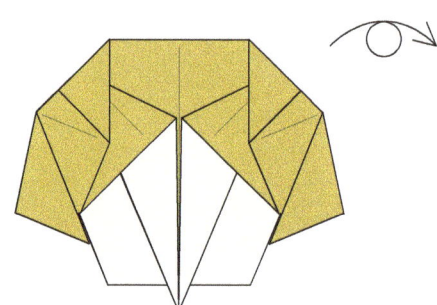

4. Turn over.

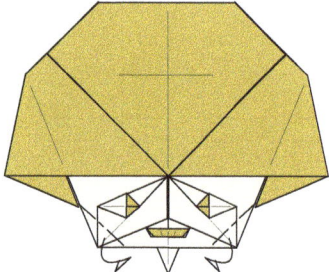

5. Mountain fold the corners.

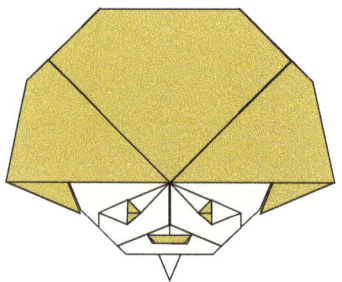

6. Completed *Detailed Face (Short Hair)*.

FORMALWEAR

formalwear

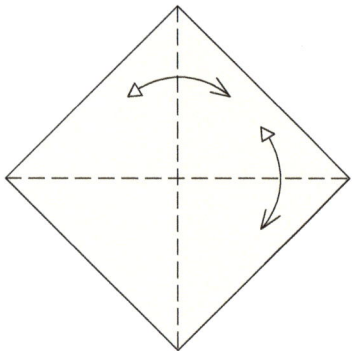

1. Precrease along the diagonals.

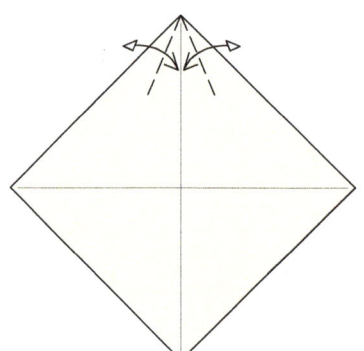

2. Precrease along the angle bisectors partway.

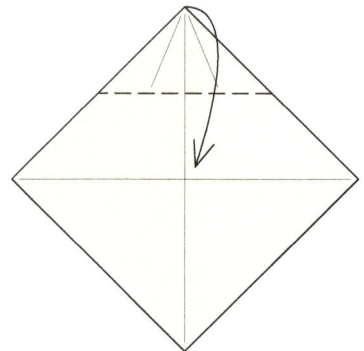

3. Valley fold the corner to the center.

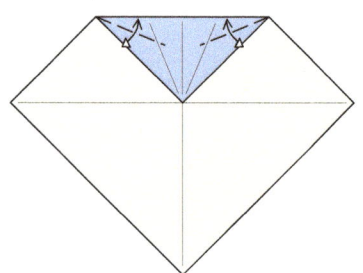

4. Precrease along the angle bisectors.

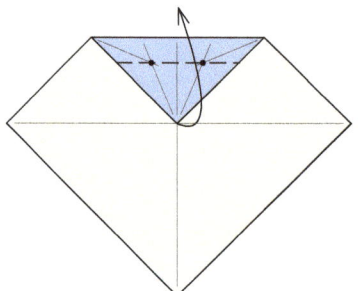

5. Valley fold through the dotted intersections.

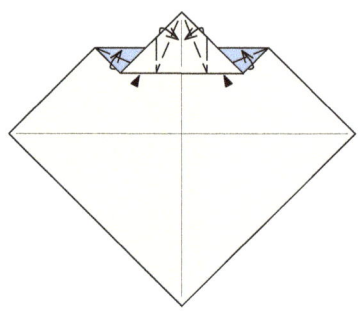

6. Swivel fold the sides along the existing creases.

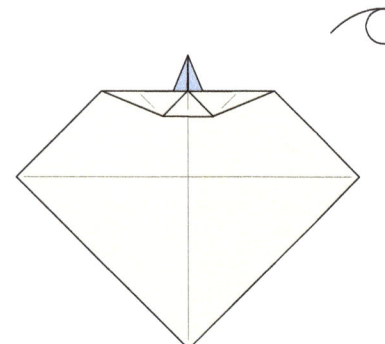

7. Turn over.

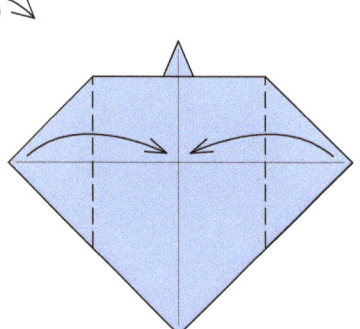

8. Valley fold the corners to the center.

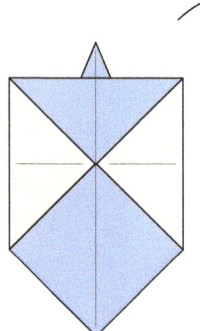

9. Turn over.

formalwear

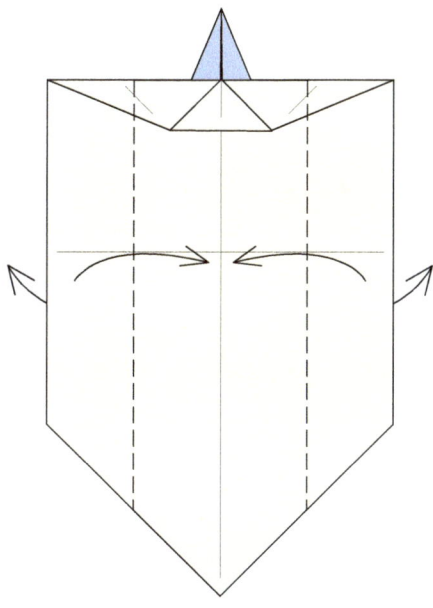

10. Valley fold the sides to the center, allowing the flaps from behind to swing forward.

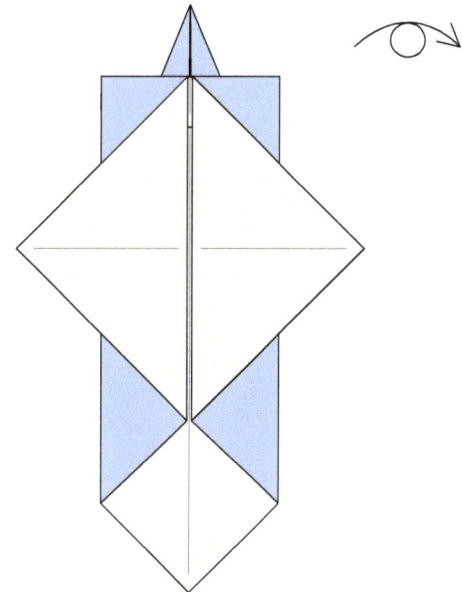

11. Turn over.

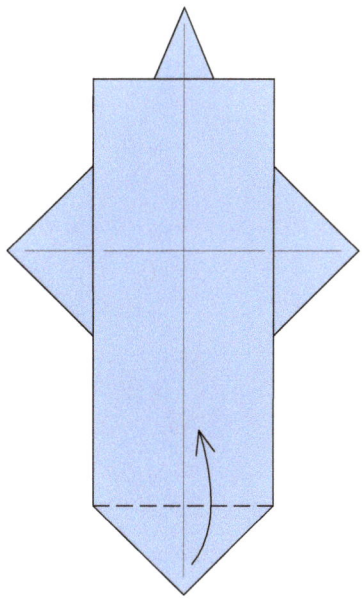

12. Valley fold the corner up.

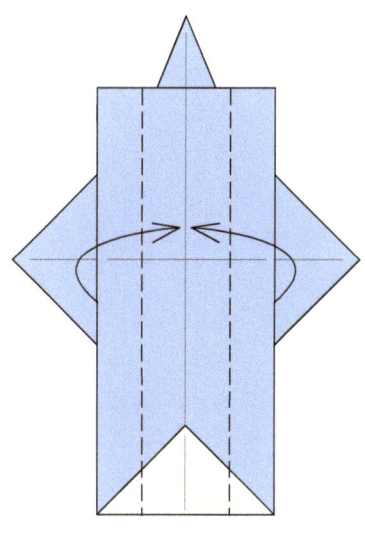

13. Valley fold the sides to the center.

formalwear

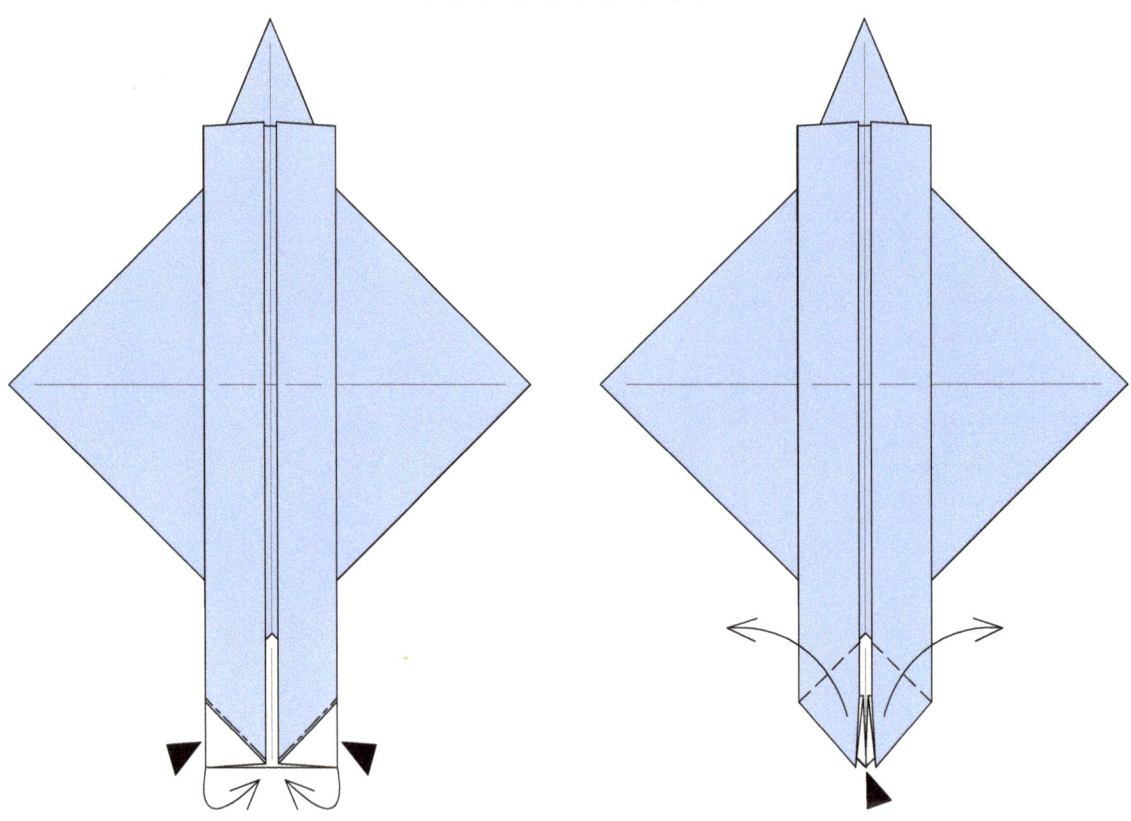

14. Reverse fold the corners.

15. Pull the side flaps outwards, allowing the center to spread apart and flatten.

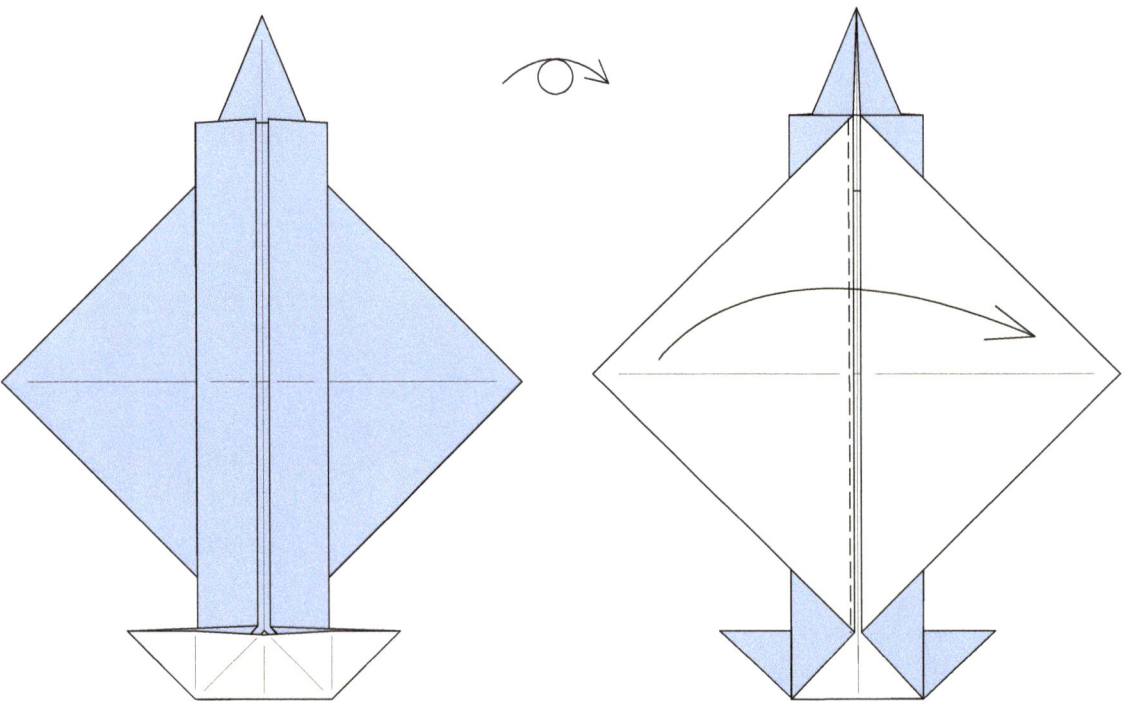

16. Turn over.

17. Swing over the top layer.

formalwear

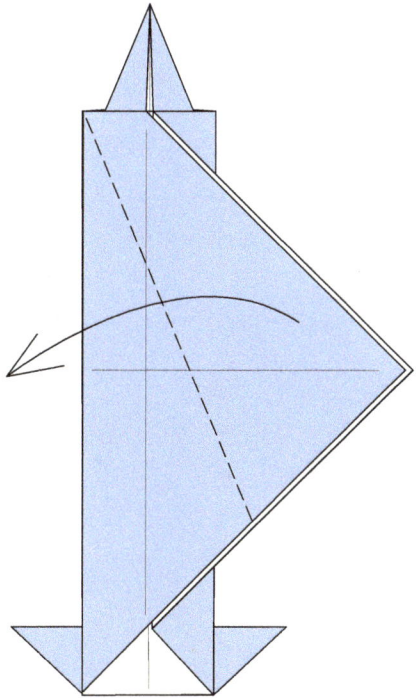

18. Valley fold the top layer over.

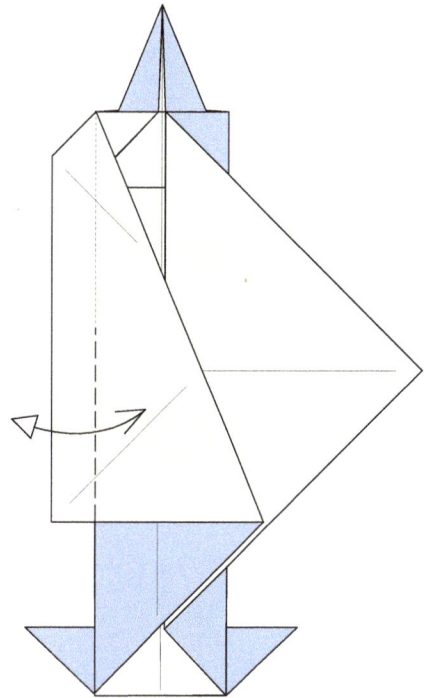

19. Precrease to align with the hidden edge.

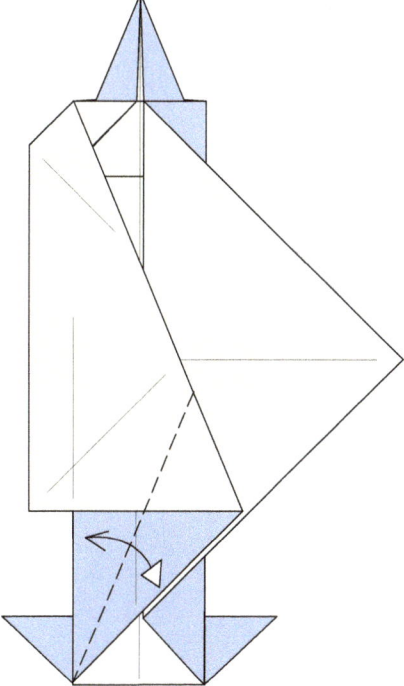

20. Precrease the top layer along the angle bisector.

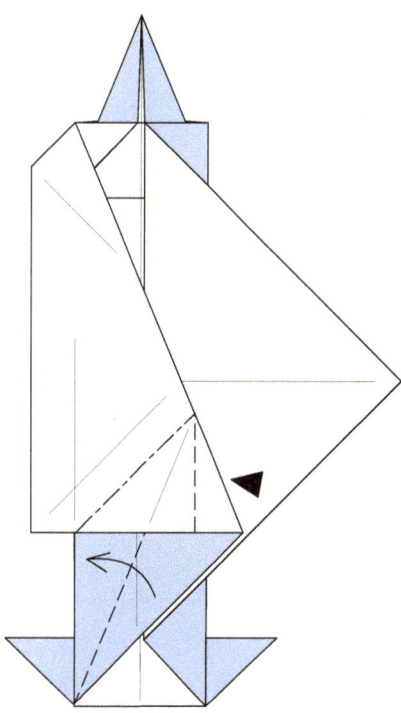

21. Reverse fold the corner along the existing creases.

formalwear

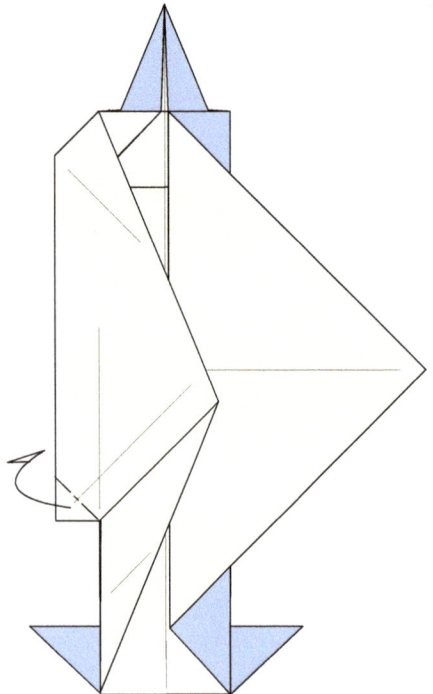

22. Mountain fold the corner.

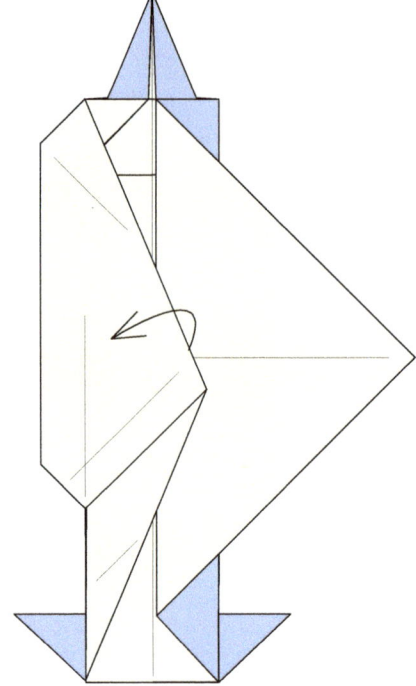

23. Tuck the flap under.

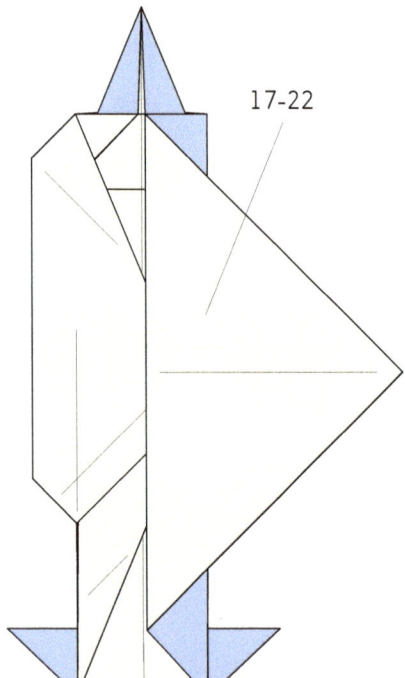

24. Repeat steps 17-22 in mirror image

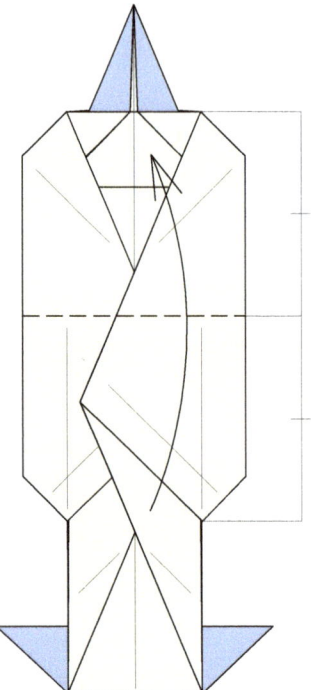

25. Valley fold the indicated section in half.

formalwear

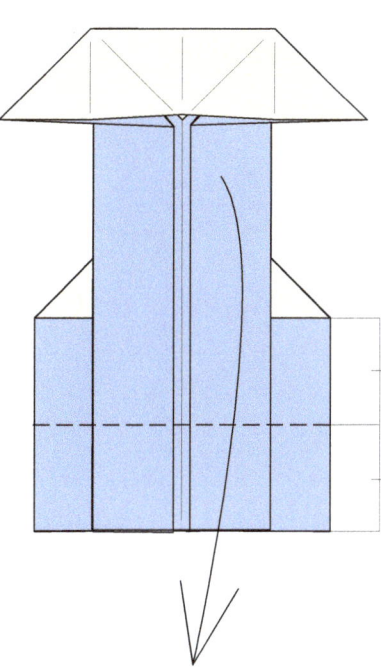

26. Valley fold the top section down, dividing the indicated portion in half.

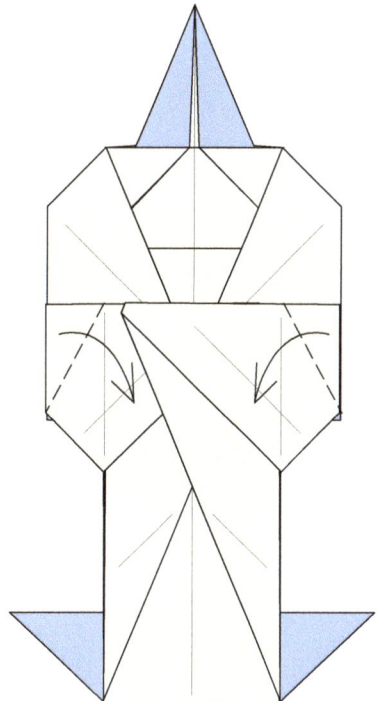

27. Valley fold the corners over.

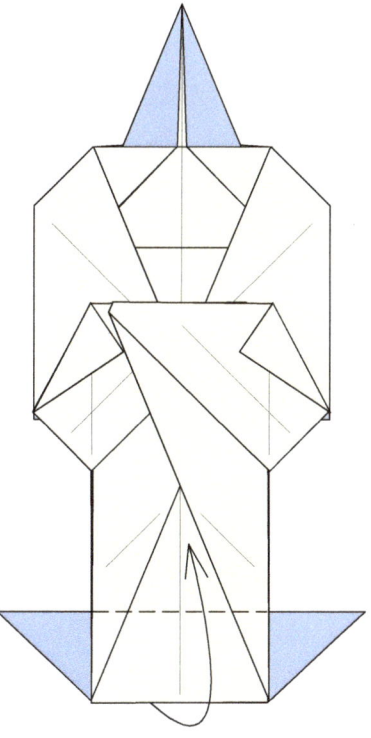

28. Valley fold the bottom section up.

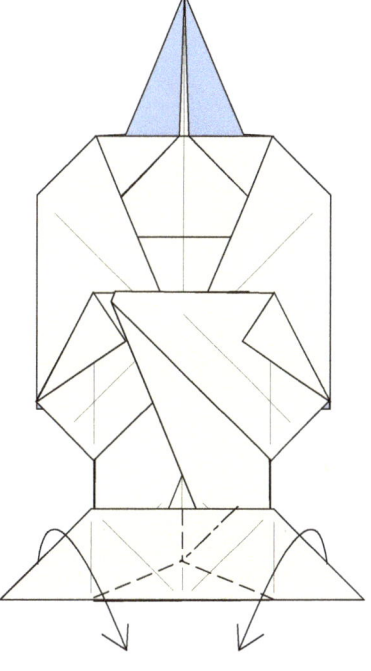

29. Form a rabbit ear fold so the bottom edges lie straight.

33

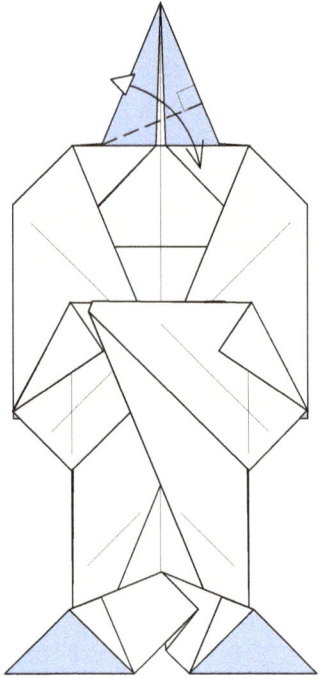

30. Precrease so the side edges align.

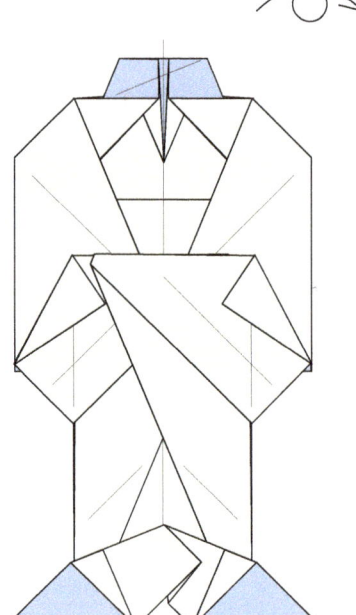

31. Reverse fold through starting from the dotted intersection.

32. Turn over.

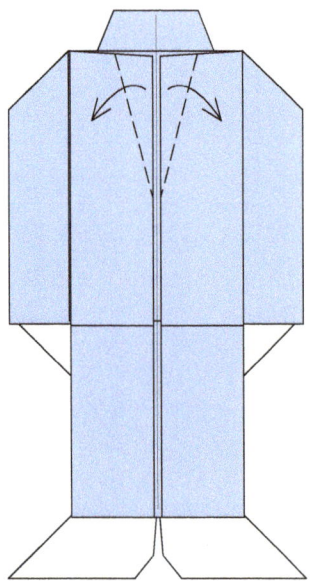

33. Valley fold the top edges outwards.

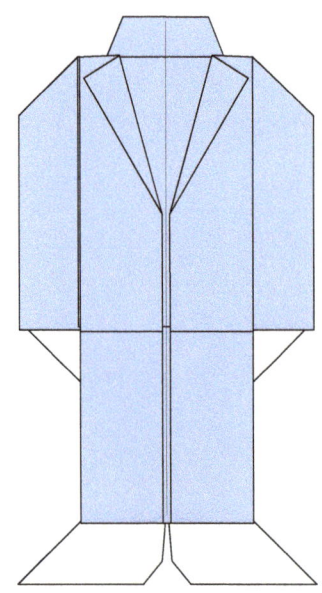

34. Insert a face into the top pocket and fold over the flap to one side to lock (see page 58 for more details).

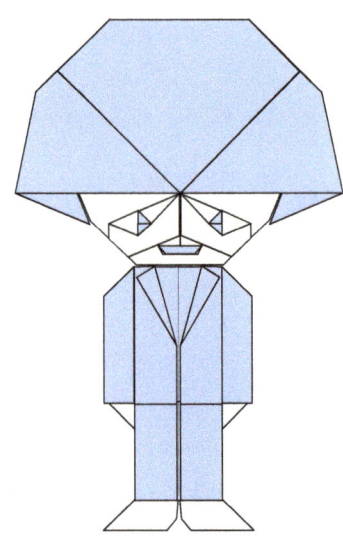

35. Completed *Formalwear*.

DRESS

dress

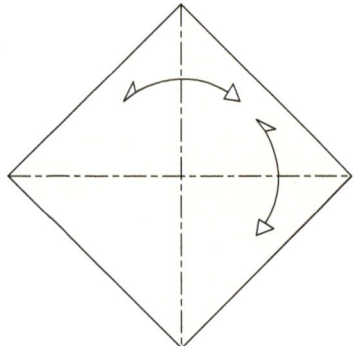

1. Precrease the diagonals with mountain folds.

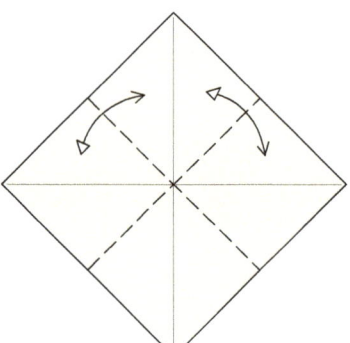

2. Precrease the sides in half.

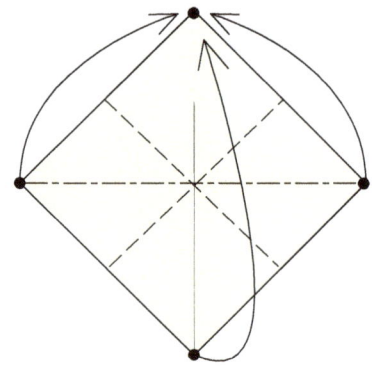

3. Collapse the corners up.

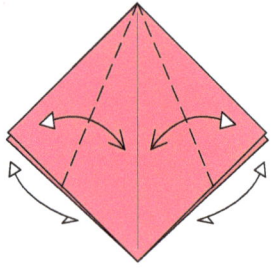

4. Precrease the sides along the angle bisectors.

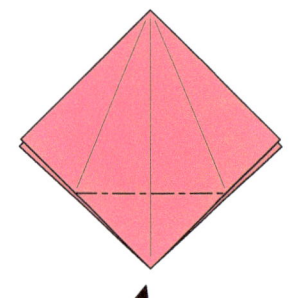

5. Sink the bottom corner.

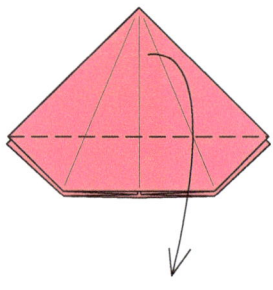

6. Valley fold the top layer.

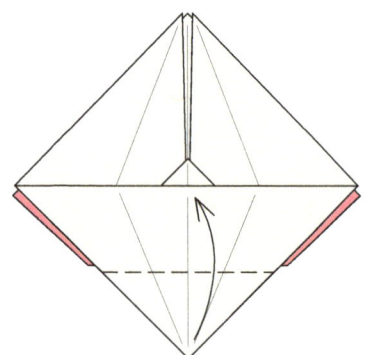

7. Valley fold to the center.

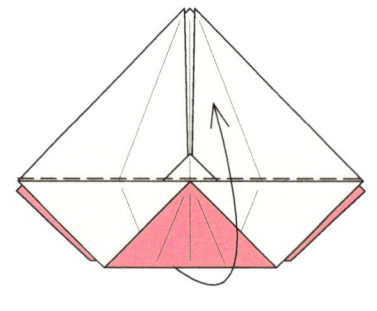

8. Swing the top flap up.

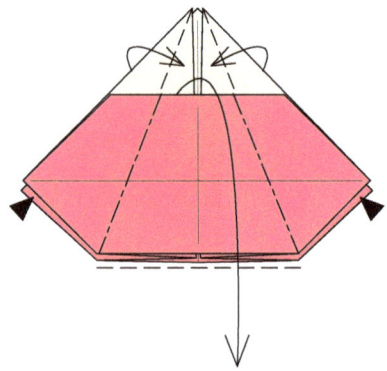

9. Petal fold the flap down.

dress

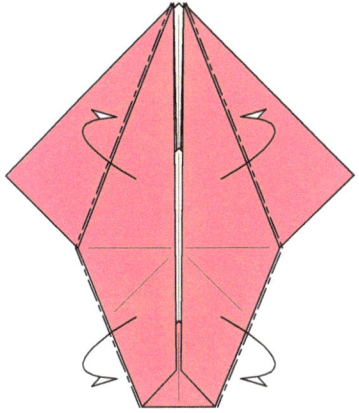

10. Wrap around a single layer at each side.

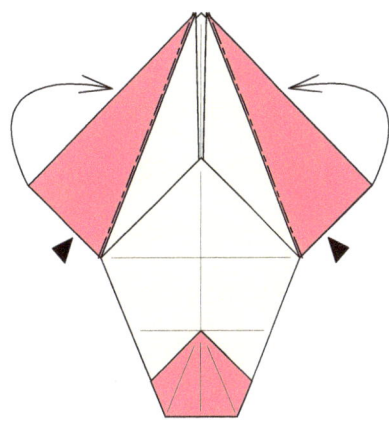

11. Reverse fold the sides.

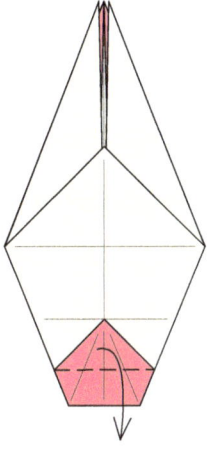

12. Valley fold the top layer.

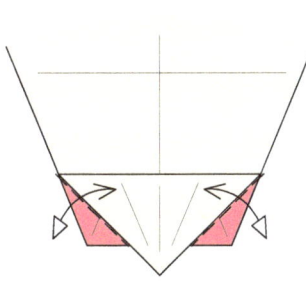

13. Precrease with mountain folds.

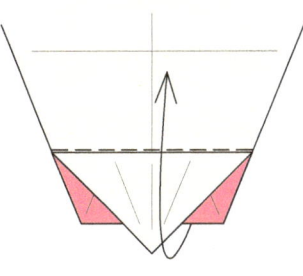

14. Valley fold the bottom section up.

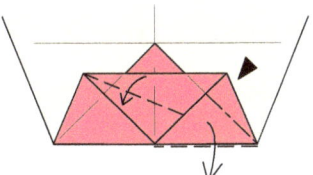

15. Squash fold along the existing creases.

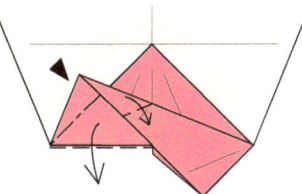

16. Squash fold the other side.

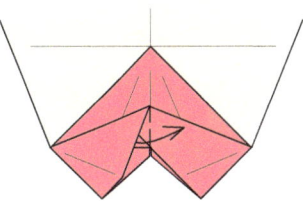

17. Pull out the trapped corner and flatten.

37

dress

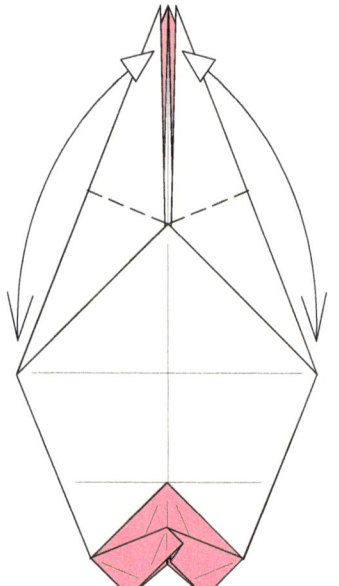

18. Precrease the top flaps.

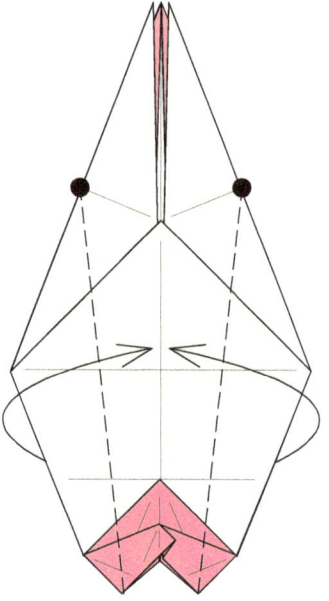

19. Valley fold the top layers starting from the dotted intersections.

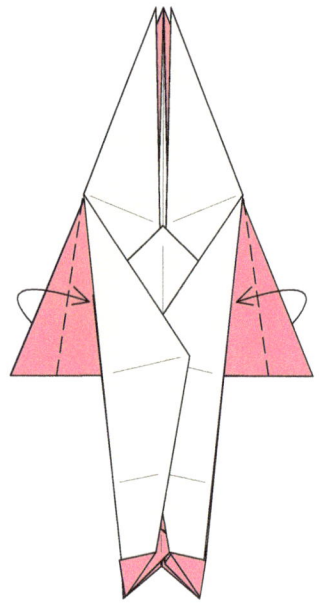

20. Valley fold along the angle bisectors.

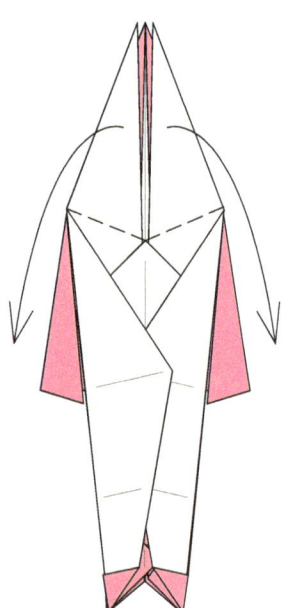

21. Valley fold along the existing creases.

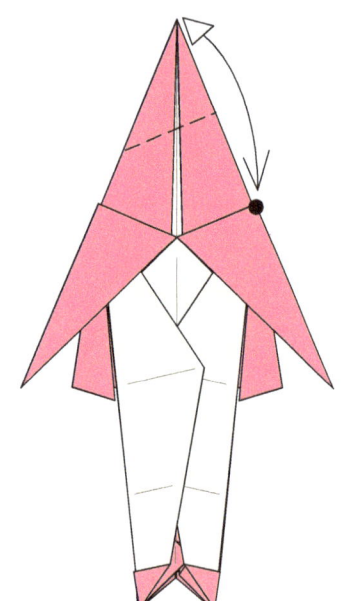

22. Valley fold to the dotted intersection.

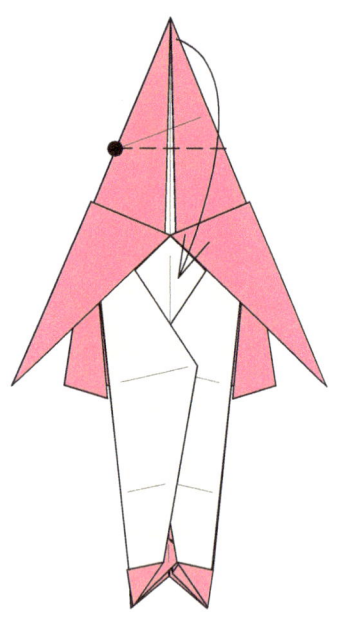

23. Valley fold starting from the dotted intersection.

dress

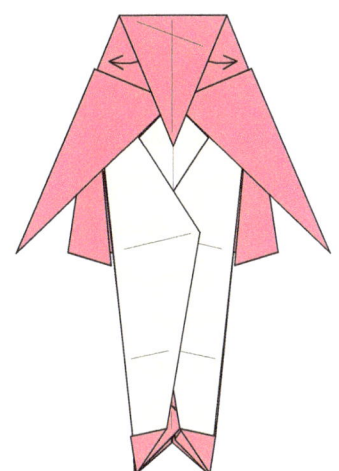

24. Slide out the side layers and flatten.

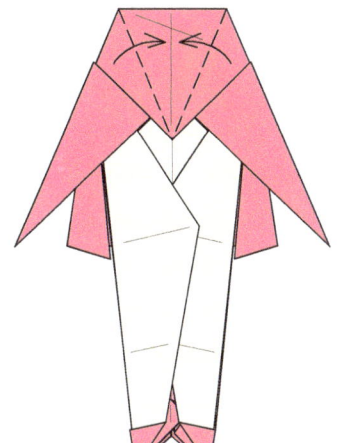

25. Valley fold the sides to the center.

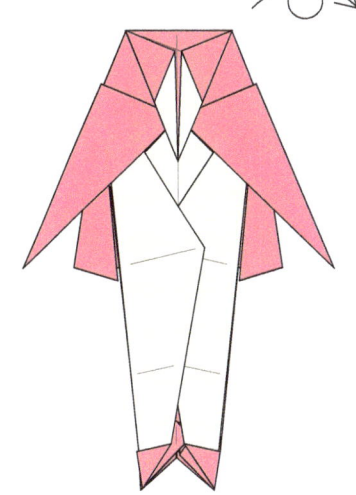

26. Turn over.

27. Insert a face into the top pocket and fold over the flap to one side to lock (see page 58 for more details).

28. Completed *Dress*.

SWIMSUIT

swimsuit

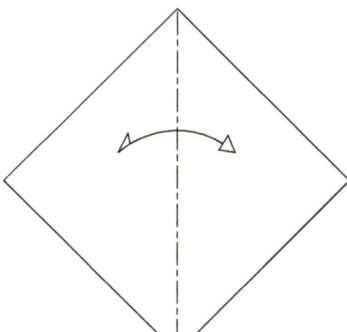

1. Precrease along the diagonal with a mountain fold.

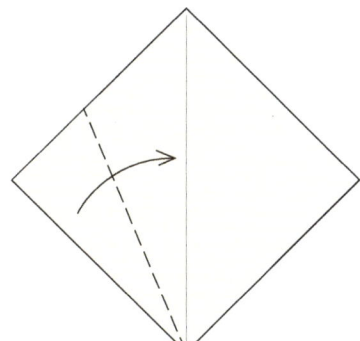

2. Valley fold along the angle bisector.

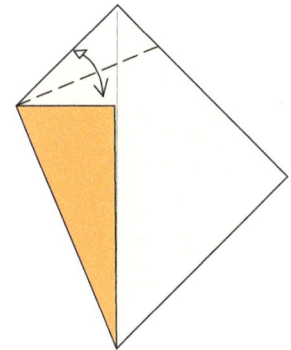

3. Precrease along the angle bisector.

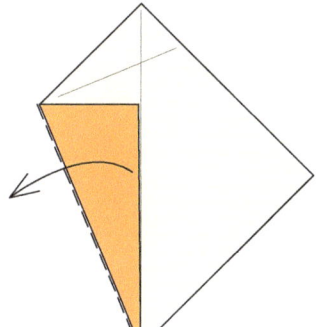

4. Open out the top layer.

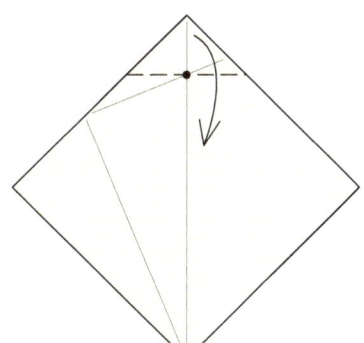

5. Valley fold through the dotted intersection.

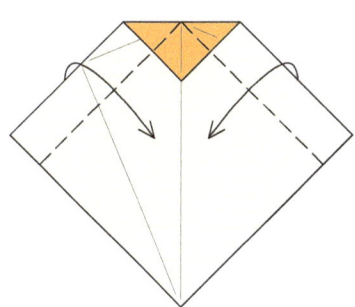

6. Valley fold the sides.

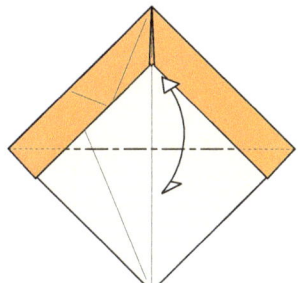

7. Precrease the single layer with a mountain fold.

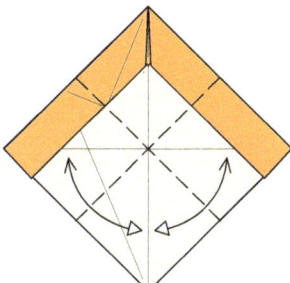

8. Precrease the sides in half.

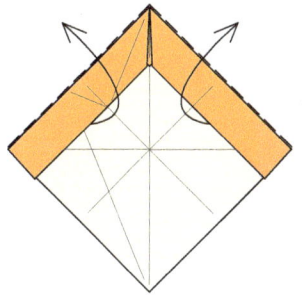

9. Open out the top edges.

41

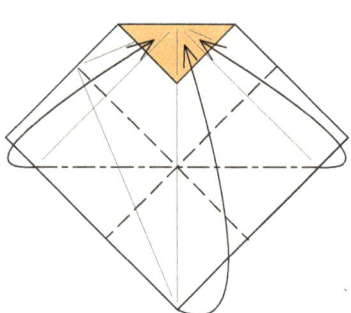

10. Bring the sides and bottom towards the top using the existing creases.

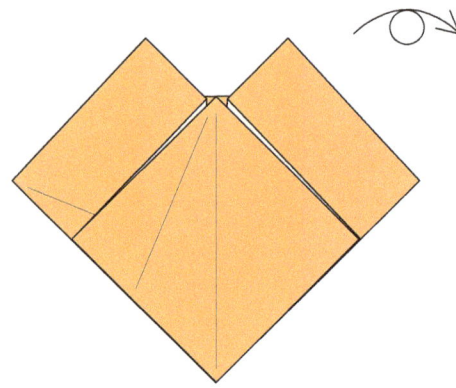

11. Turn over.

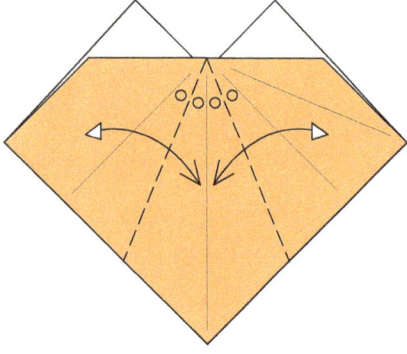

12. Precrease the top laps along the indicated angle bisectors.

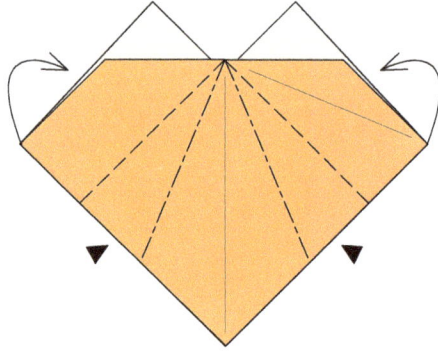

13. Reverse fold the sides in and out along the existing creases.

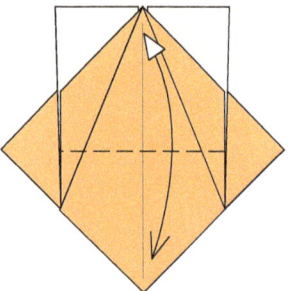

14. Precrease the top flap in half.

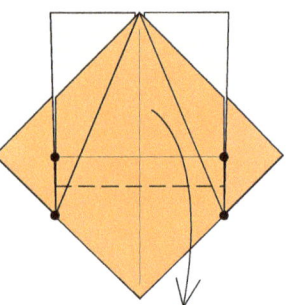

15. Valley fold the flap down, dividing the dotted region in half.

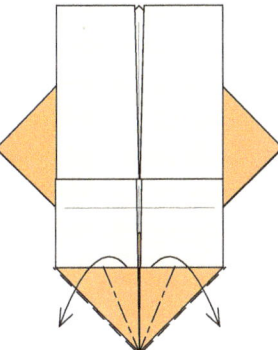

16. Pull out the top layer from each side and flatten.

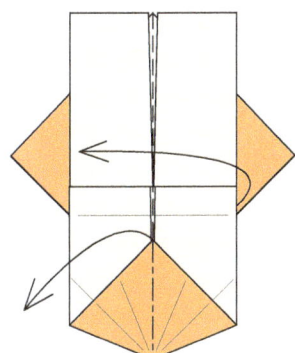

17. Swing the top layer over while opening out the corner.

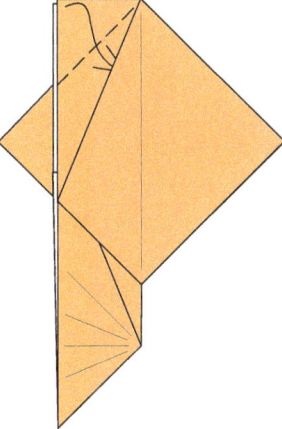

18. Valley fold the corner into the pocket.

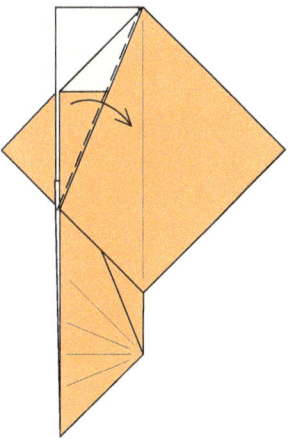

19. Valley fold the edge over.

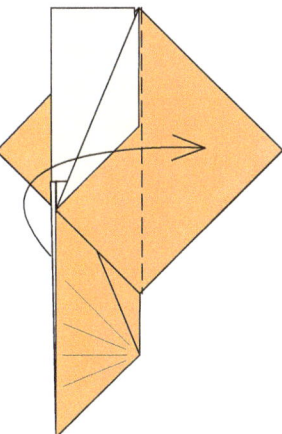

20. Swing the flap over.

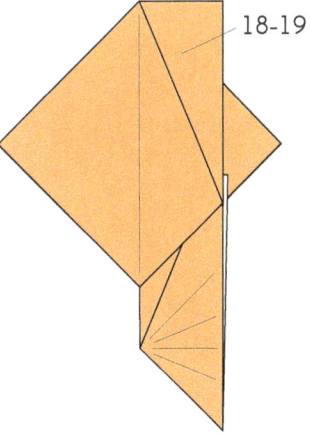

21. Repeat steps 18-19 in mirror image.

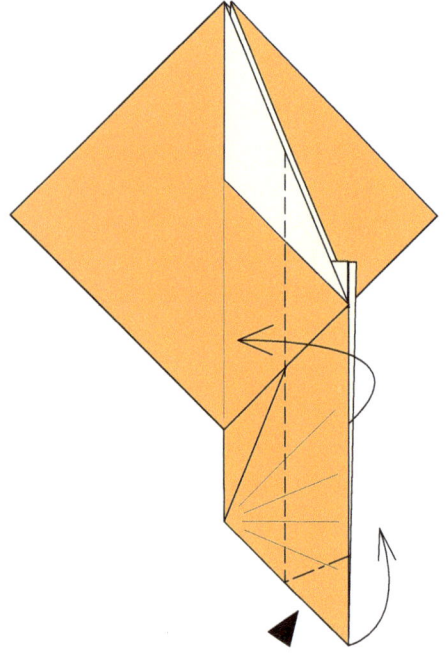

22. Valley fold over one layer while squash folding the bottom corner.

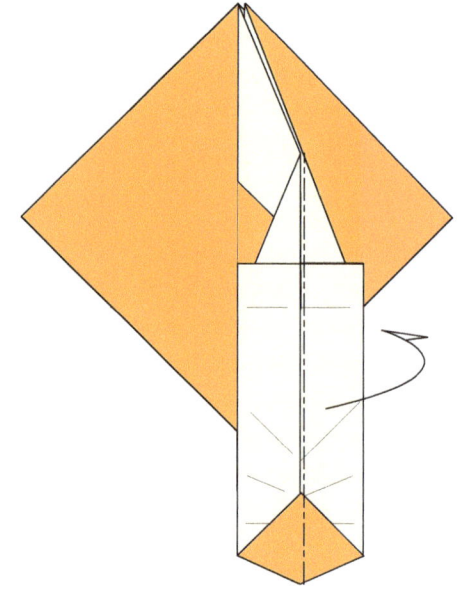

23. Mountain fold the edge behind.

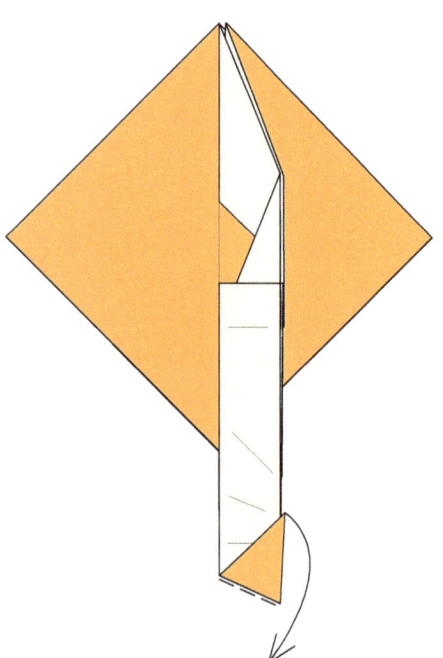

24. Wrap around the outer layer and flatten.

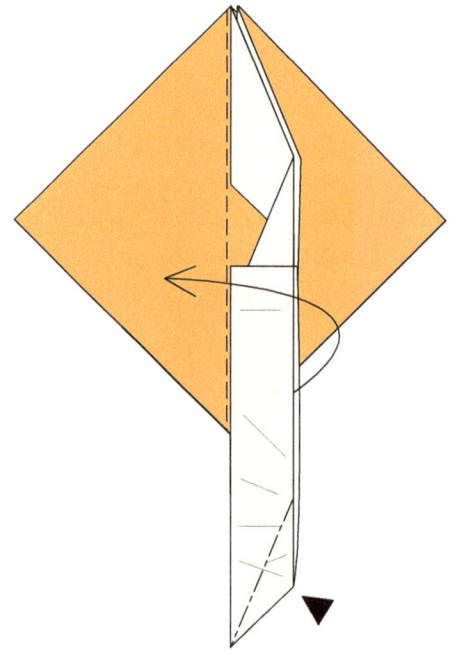

25. Spread the flap apart while spread squashing the bottom corner.

swimsuit

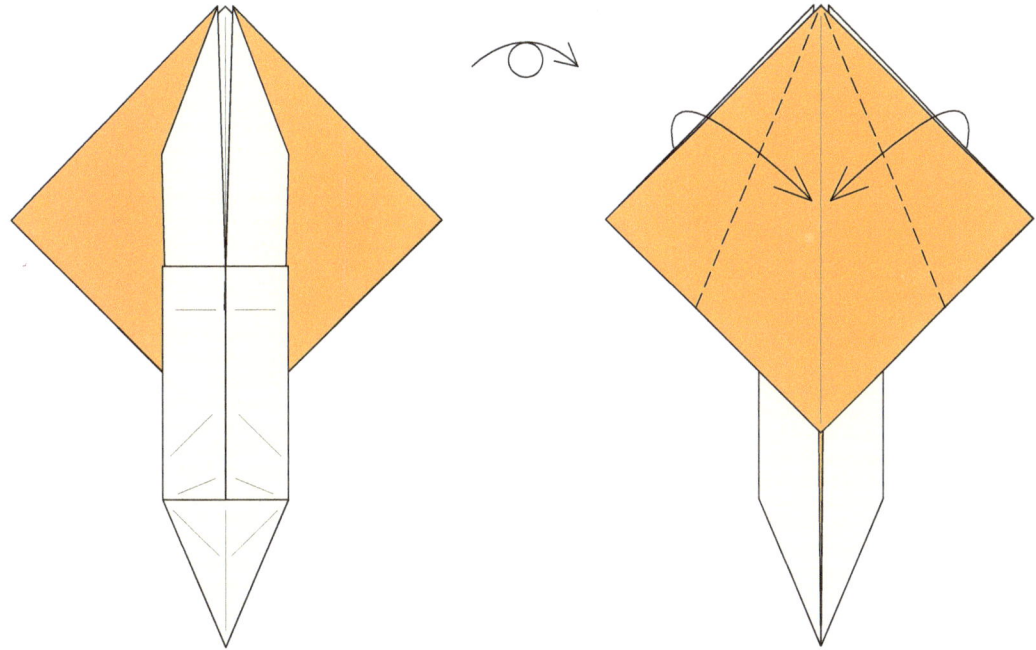

26. Turn over.

27. Valley fold the sides to the center.

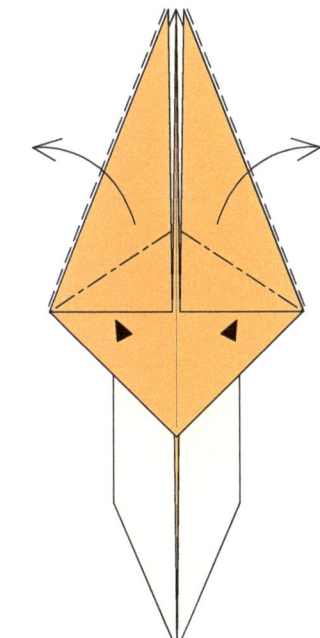

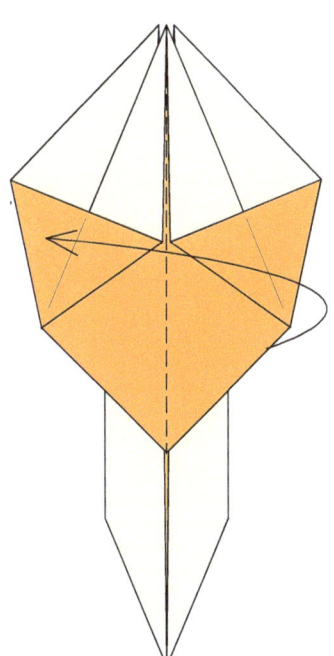

28. Squash fold the top flaps.

29. Swing over the side flap.

45

swimsuit

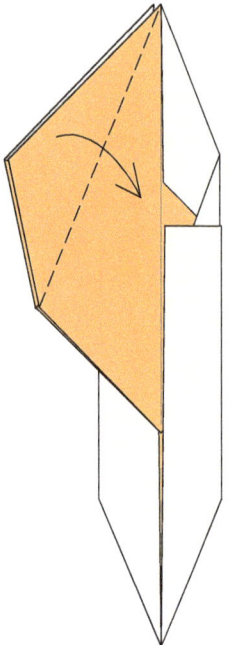

30. Valley fold the top layer.

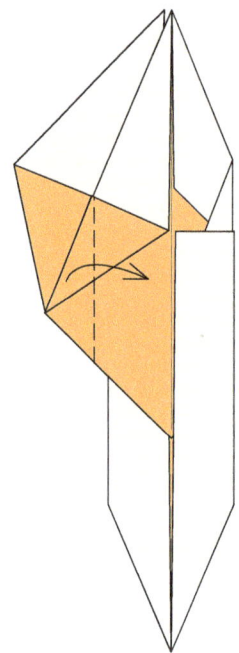

31. Valley fold the corner in partway.

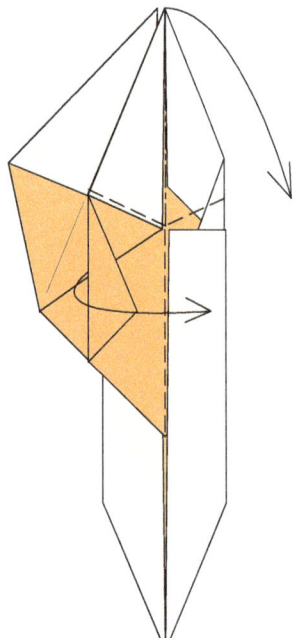

32. Close the flap up while reverse folding the top point down.

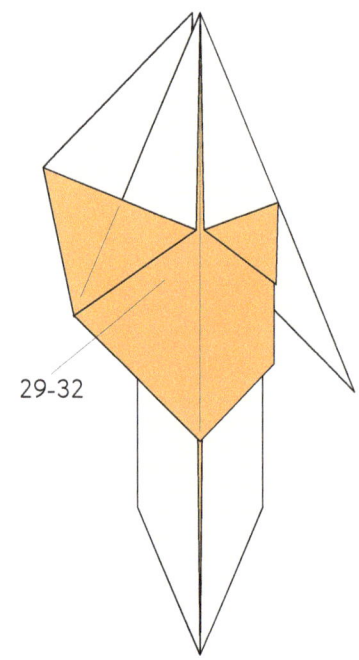

29-32

33. Repeat steps 29-32 in mirror image.

swimsuit

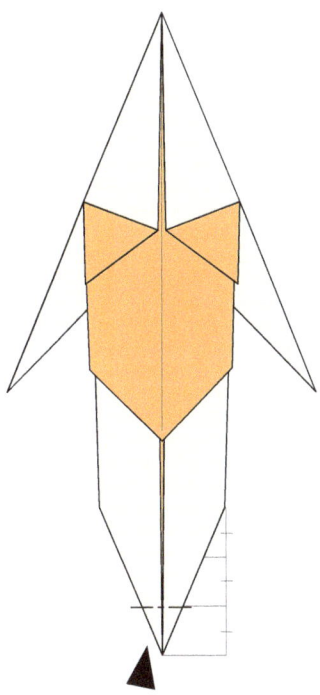

34. Reverse fold the corner in at about 1/3rd the indicated height.

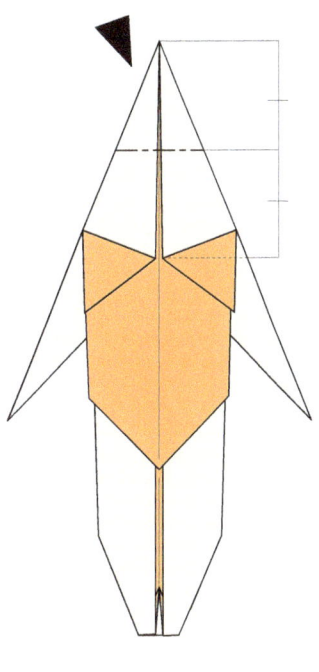

35. Reverse fold the top corner in halfway.

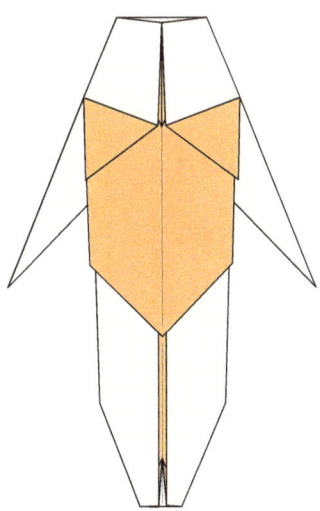

36. Insert a face into the top pocket and fold over the flap to one side to lock (see page 58 for more details).

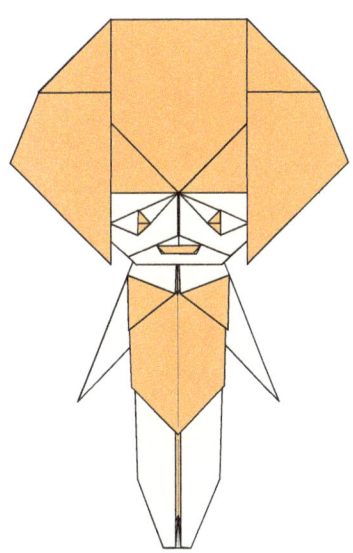

37. Completed *Swimsuit*.

CASUALWEAR

casualwear

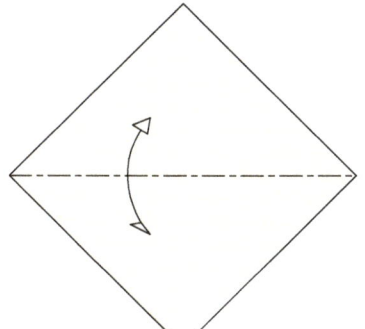

1. Precrease along the diagonal with a mountain fold.

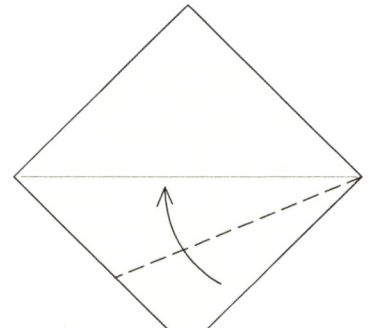

2. Valley fold along the angle bisector.

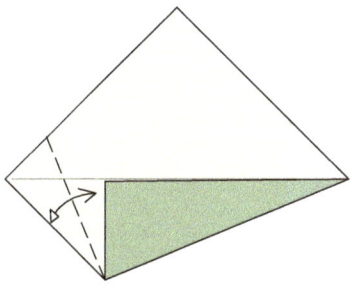

3. Precrease along the angle bisector.

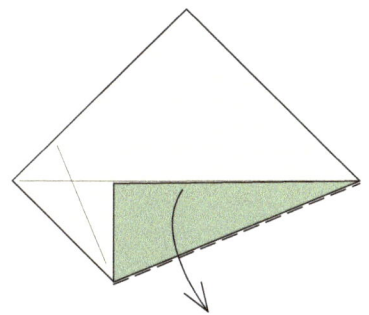

4. Unfold the top layer.

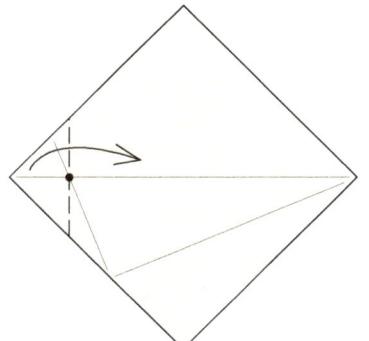

5. Valley fold through the dotted intersection of creases.

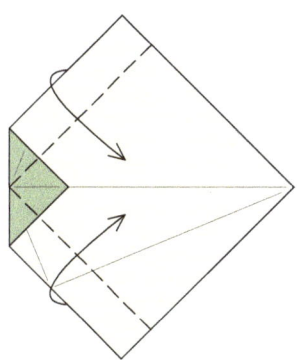

6. Valley fold the sides.

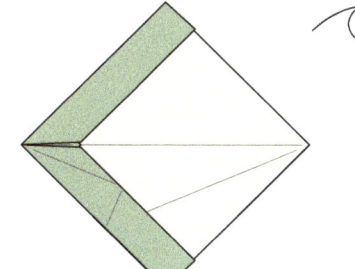

7. Turn over.

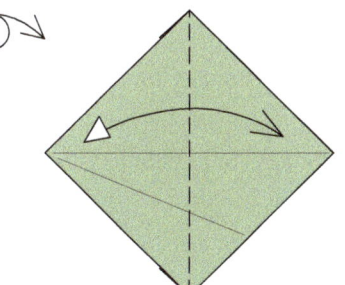

8. Precrease in half.

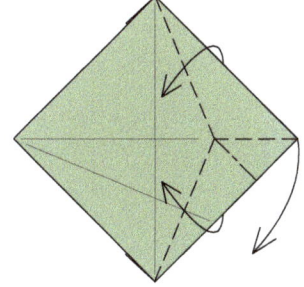

9. Rabbit ear one side.

casualwear

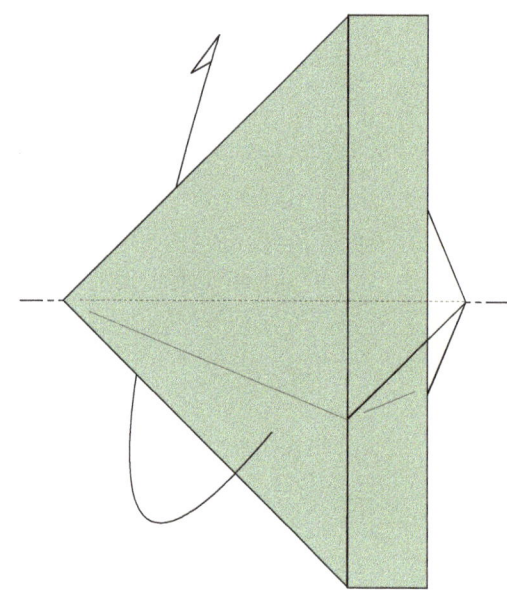

10. Mountain fold in half.

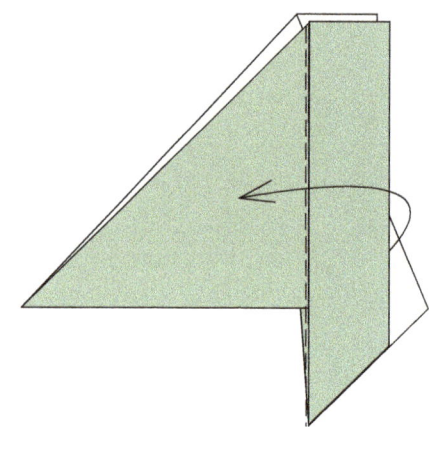

11. Swing over the top layer.

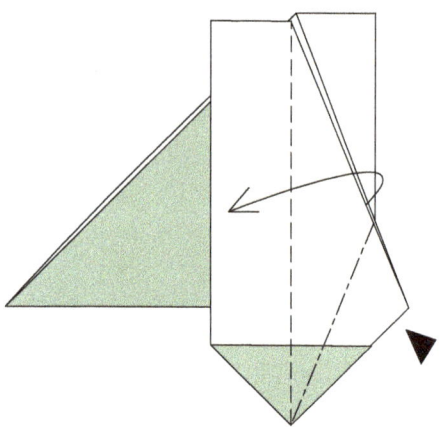

12. Spread squash the flap.

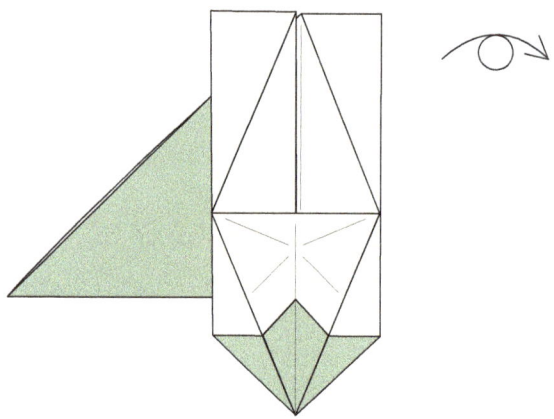

13. Turn over.

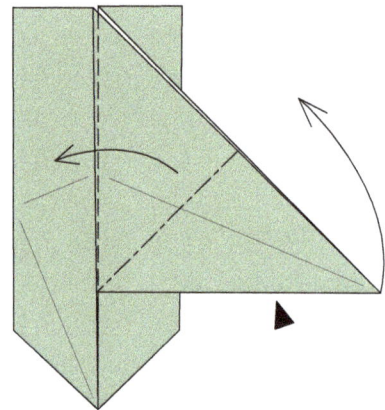

14. Squash fold the flap.

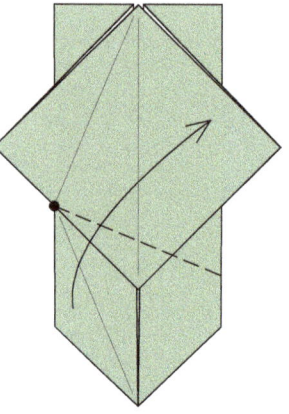

15. Starting from the dotted intersection, valley fold the flap over.

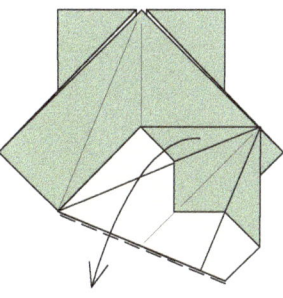

16. Note how the top edge of the flap lies straight. Unfold the flap.

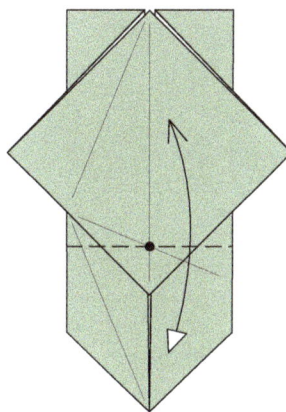

17. Precrease through the dotted intersection of creases.

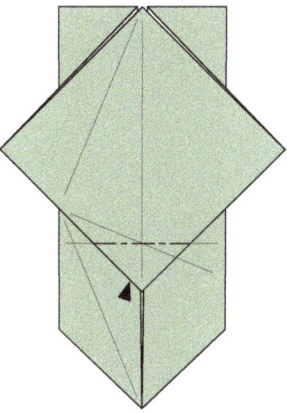

18. Sink the trapped flap.

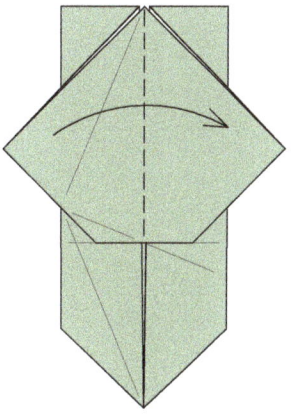

19. Swing over one layer.

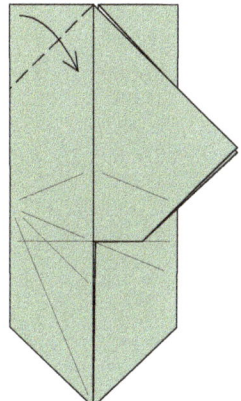

20. Valley fold the corner.

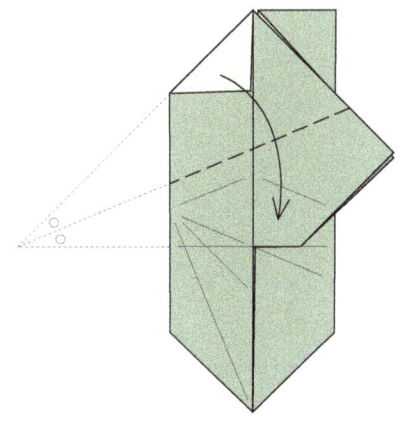

21. Valley fold along the imaginary angle bisector.

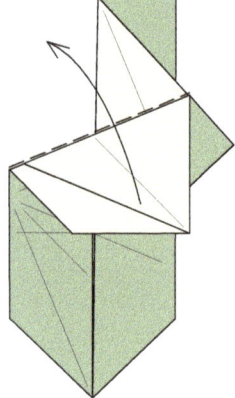

22. Unfold the flap.

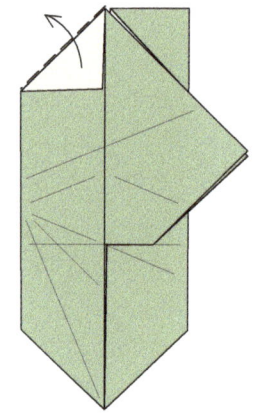

23. Unfold the corner.

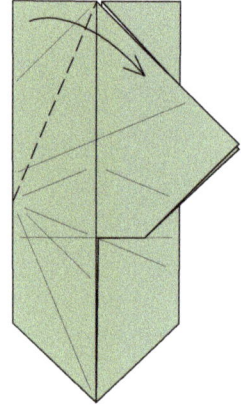

24. Valley fold so the crease aligns with the center.

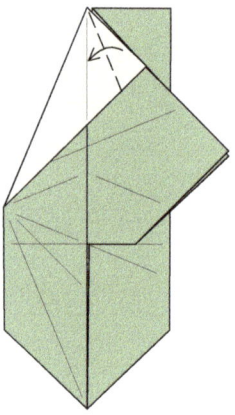

25. Valley fold to the crease.

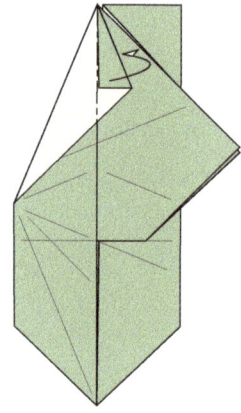

26. Mountain fold along the existing crease.

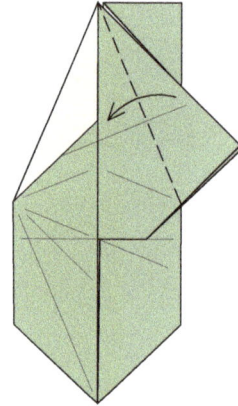

27. Valley fold along the angle bisector.

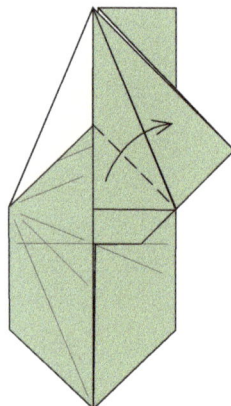

28. Valley fold the flap so its side lies straight.

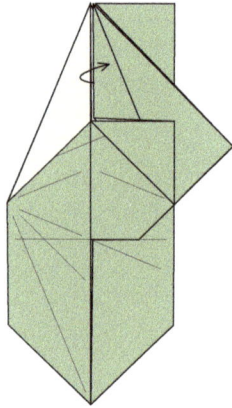

29. Bring the flap to the surface.

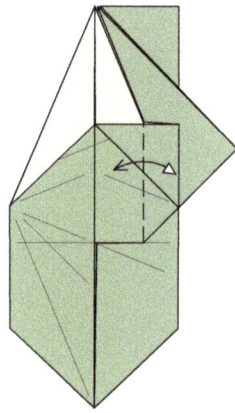

30. Precrease the flap partway.

casualwear

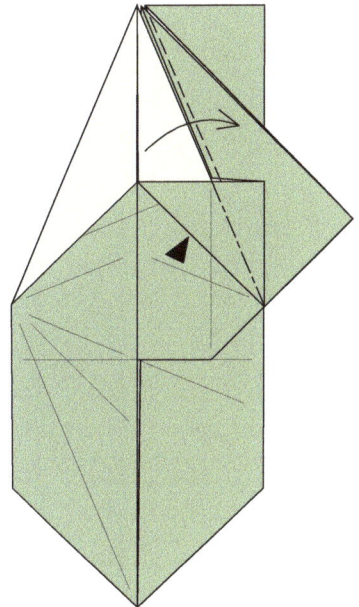

31. Squash fold the flap.

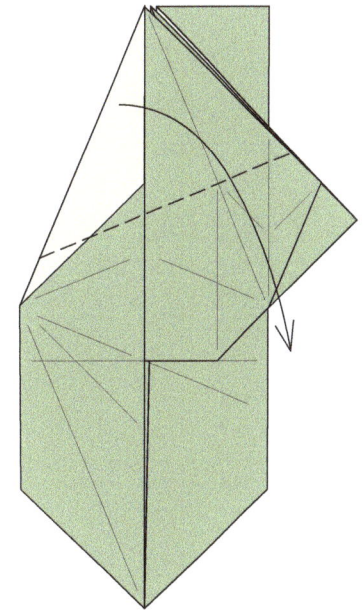

32. Valley fold along the existing crease.

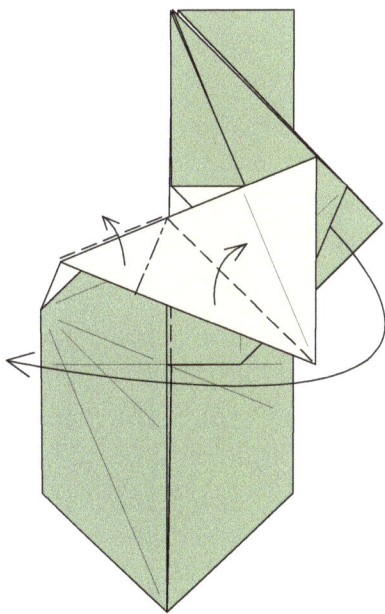

33. Valley fold the flap over while swivel folding the edge up.

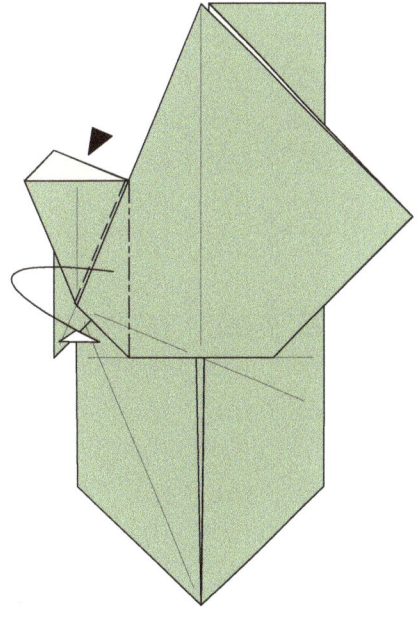

34. Swivel fold the side in along the existing crease.

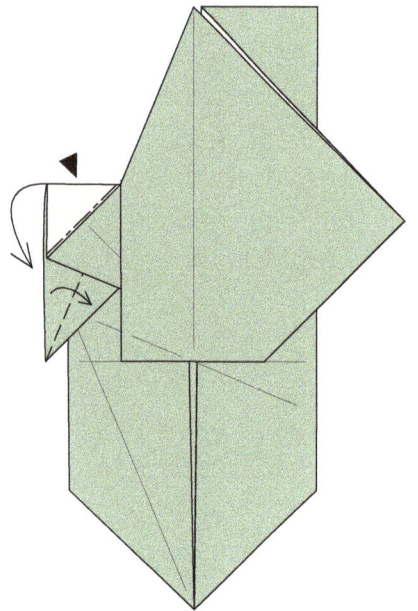

35. Swivel fold along the angle bisector.

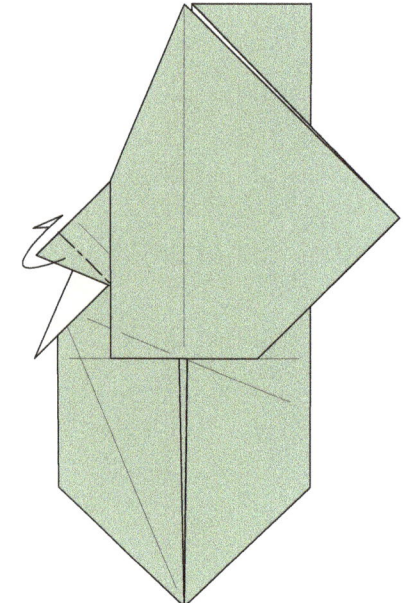

36. Mountain fold the corner.

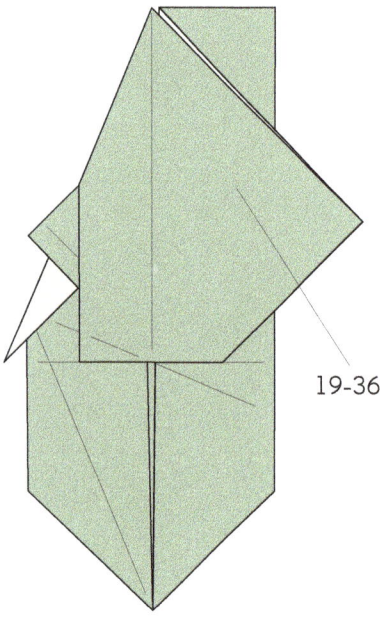

37. Repeat steps 19-36 in mirror image.

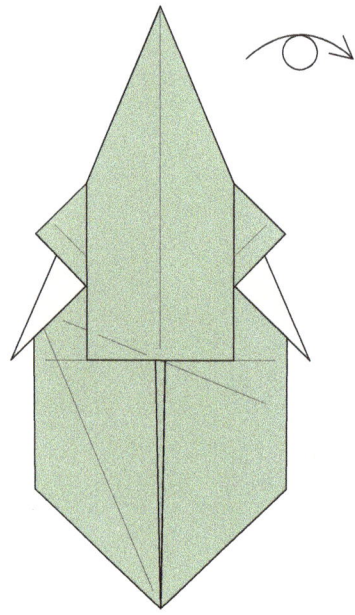

38. Turn over.

casualwear

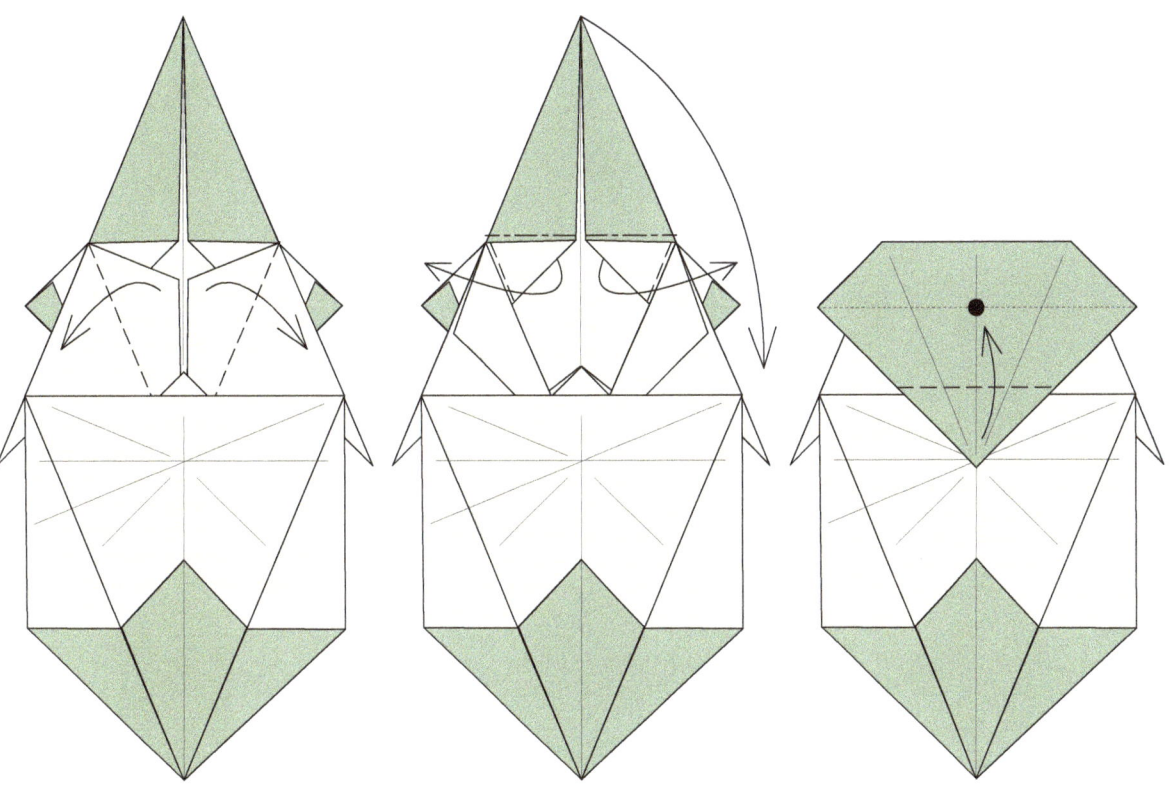

39. Valley fold the flaps outwards.

40. Bring the flap down while spreading the side layers open.

41. Valley fold to the imaginary dotted intersection.

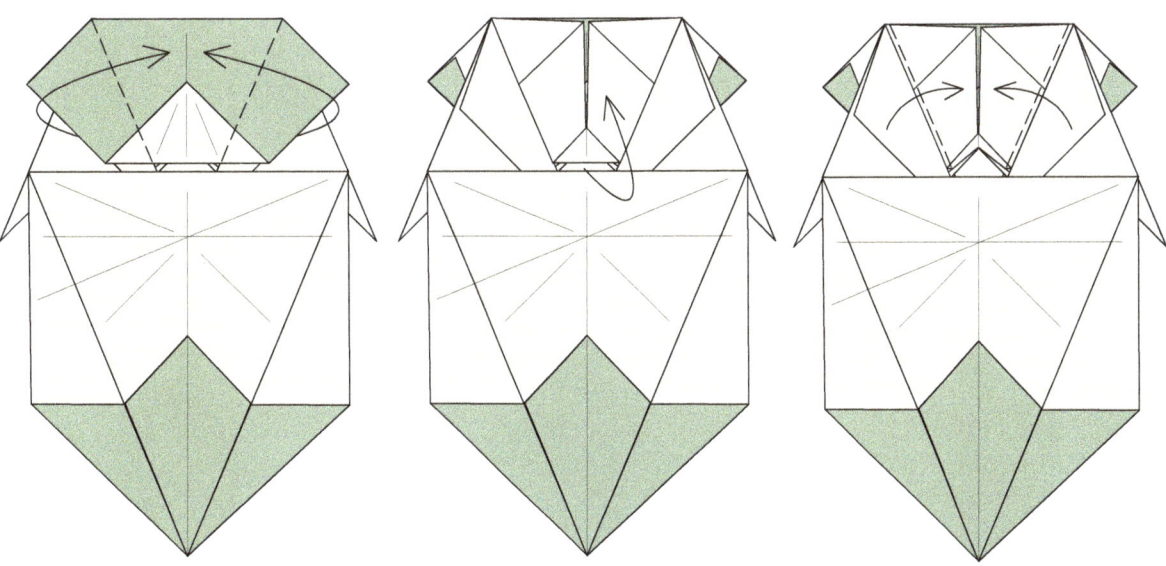

42. Valley fold the sides to the center.

43. Tuck the tip of the flap under.

44. Swing the side flaps back.

casualwear

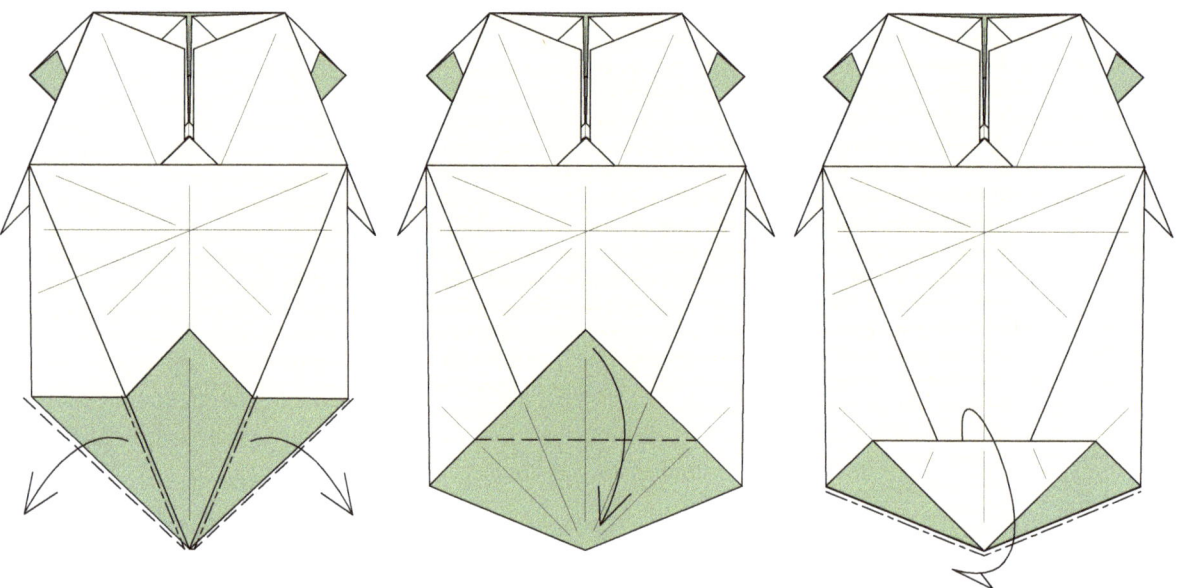

45. Slide out the side layers.

46. Valley fold the corner down.

47. Wrap around the top layer.

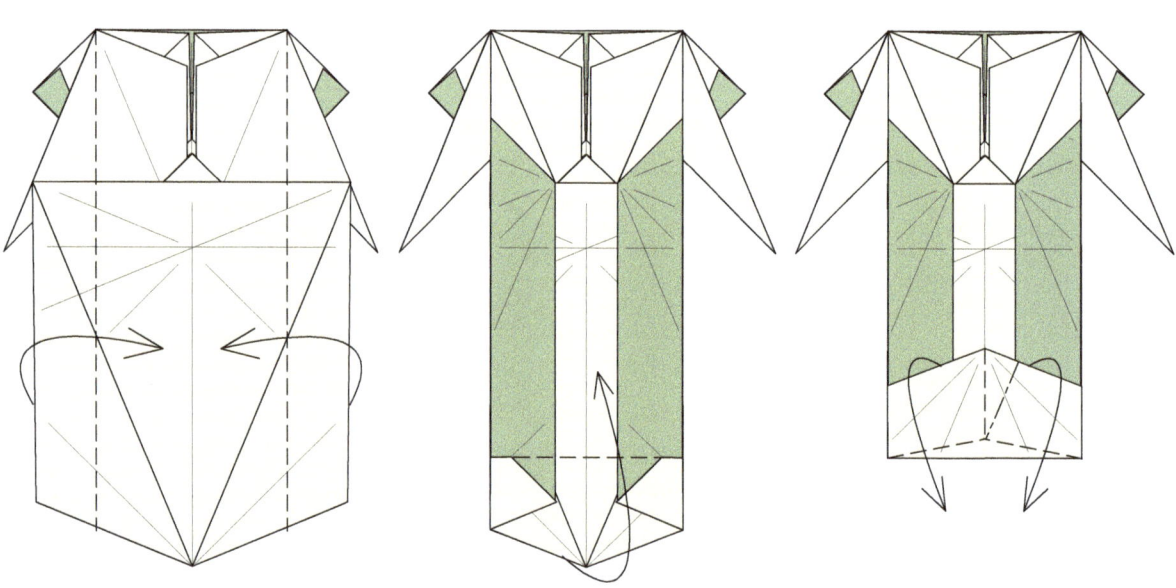

48. Valley fold the sides.

49. Valley fold the bottom edge.

50. Form a shallow rabbit ear fold so the bottom edges lie straight.

casualwear

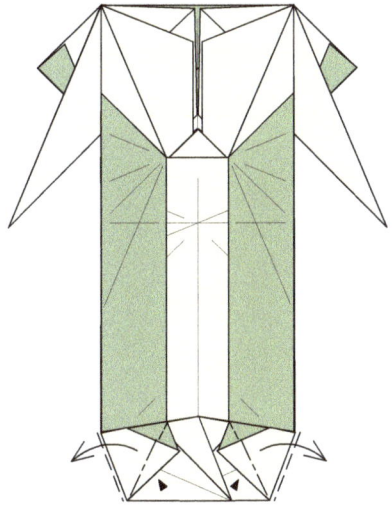

51. Slide out the top layer at each side.

52. Fold the corner up, allowing the sides to squash fold.

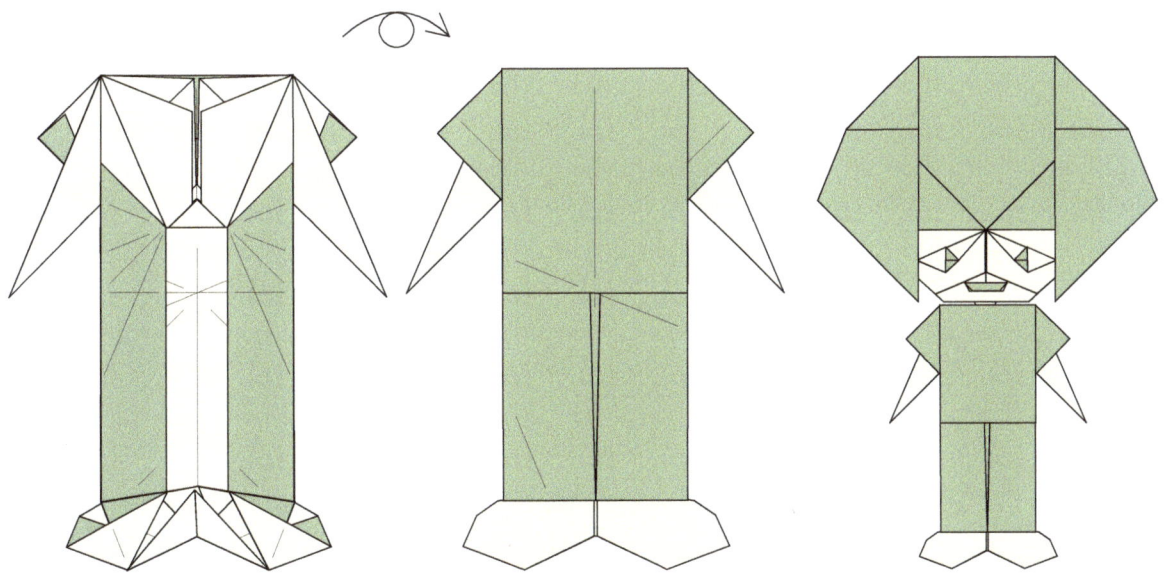

53. Turn over.

54. Insert a face into the top pocket and fold over the flap to one side to lock (see page 58 for more details).

55. Completed *Casualwear*.

57

FACE TO BODY ATTACHMENT

These steps describe the general approach to attaching any of the four heads to any of the four bodies. The *Swimsuit* attachment is slightly different as the locking procedure (step three) happens on the front of the model. So, for that model you do not turn over in step one and in step four.

All the tabs and pockets will vary in size slightly. This should give you some flexibility in how the heads are positioned on the bodies. The connections will still work if you use papers that are close enough in size (about 20% difference between the starting sheets should give enough material to make a connection).

Until you make the final lock, the attachments are loose, but will stay together securely. It is very easy to undo the lock and swap out another head or body piece. Of course, for an even more permanent attachment you can use glue.

face to body attachment

1. Begin with one of the heads and one of the bodies. Turn over.

2. Tuck the tab from the head into the pocket from the body to the desired height.

3. Valley fold the hidden cluster of flaps over to lock into place.

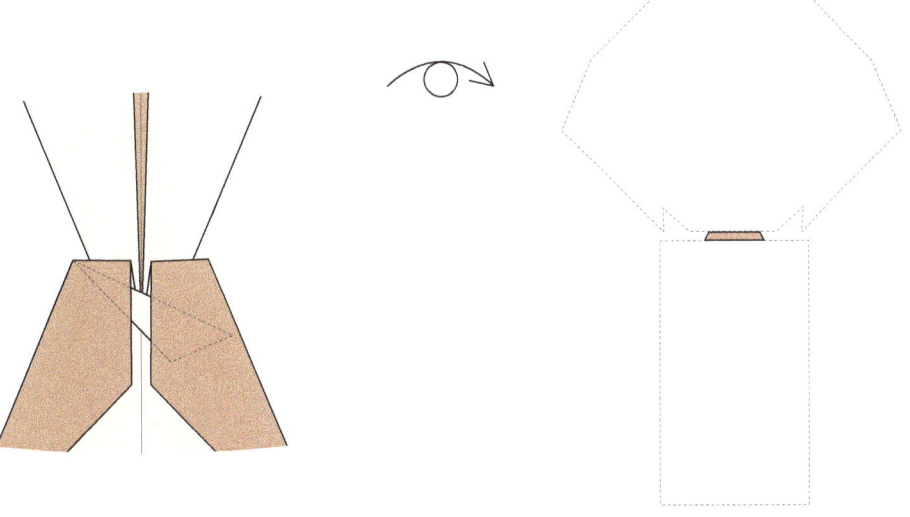

4. Turn over.

5. Completed *Face to Body Attachment*.

ANGEL

angel

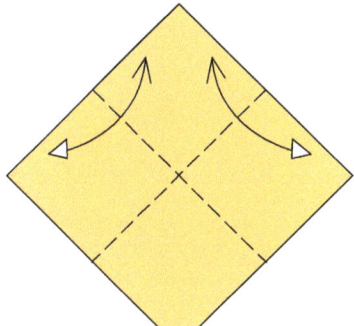

1. Precrease the sides in half.

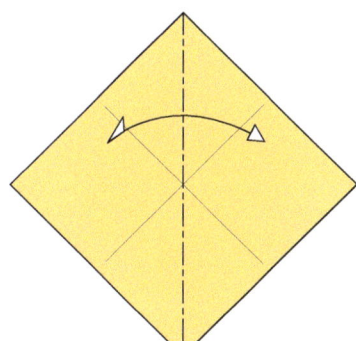

2. Precrease along the diagonal with a mountain fold.

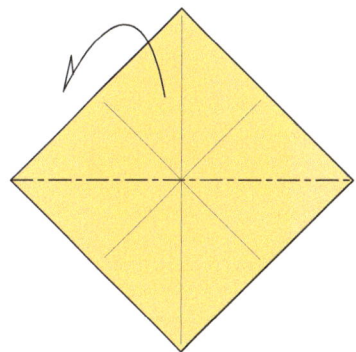

3. Mountain fold along the diagonal.

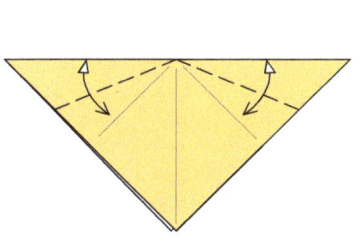

4. Precrease along the angle bisectors.

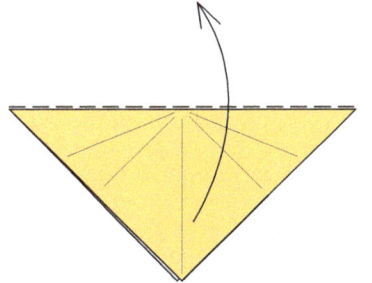

5. Open out completely.

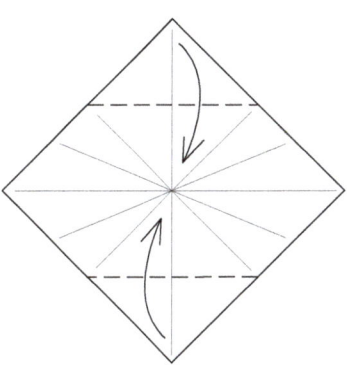

6. Valley fold the corners to the center.

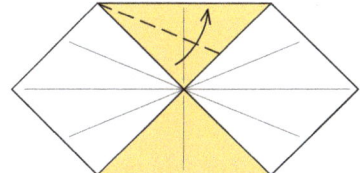

7. Lightly valley fold along the angle bisector.

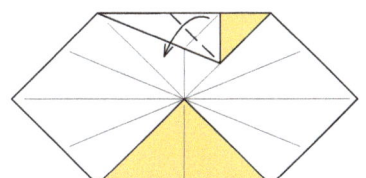

8. Valley fold the corner over.

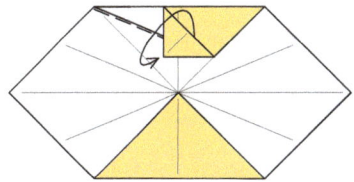

9. Swing the edge down, tucking the corner inside.

angel

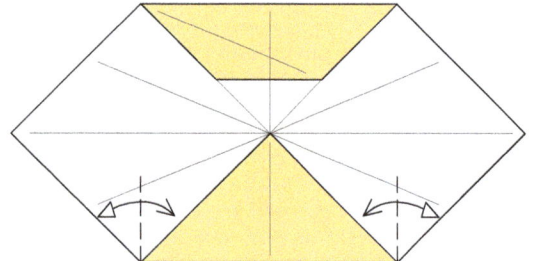

10. Precrease the bottom corners partway.

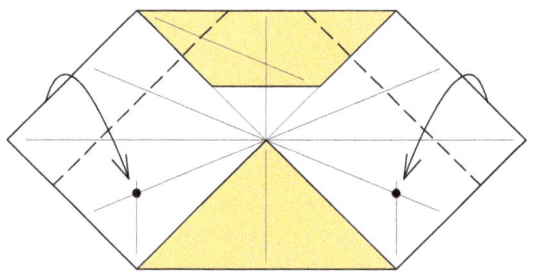

11. Valley fold the edges towards the dotted intersections of creases.

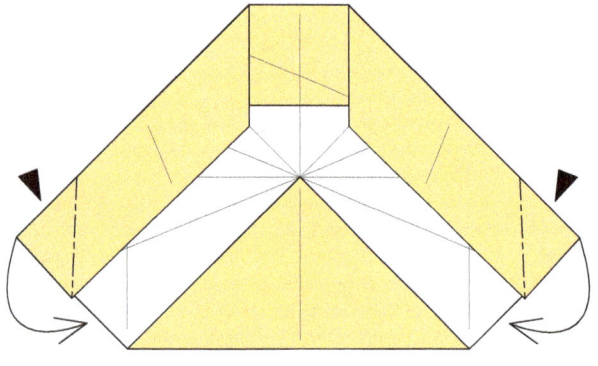

12. Reverse fold the corners.

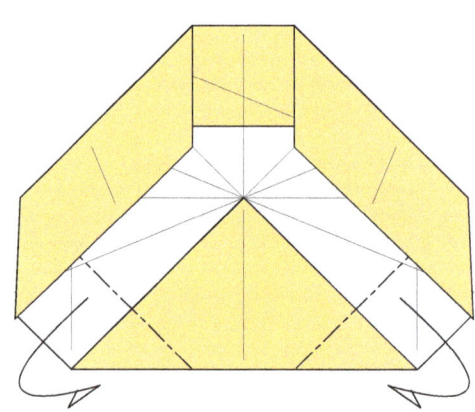

13. Mountain fold the edges behind.

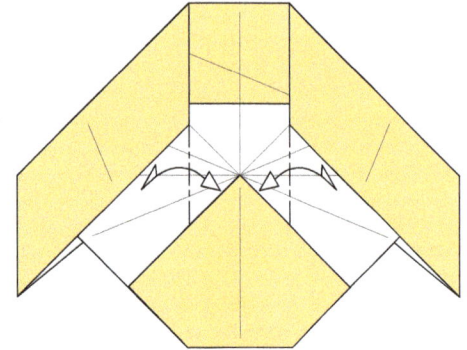

14. Precrease with mountain folds.

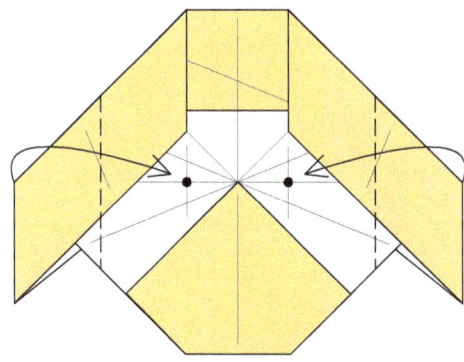

15. Valley fold to the dotted intersections of creases.

angel

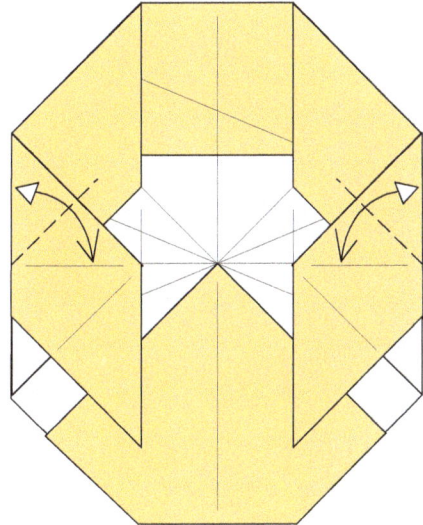

16. Precrease partway along the angle bisectors.

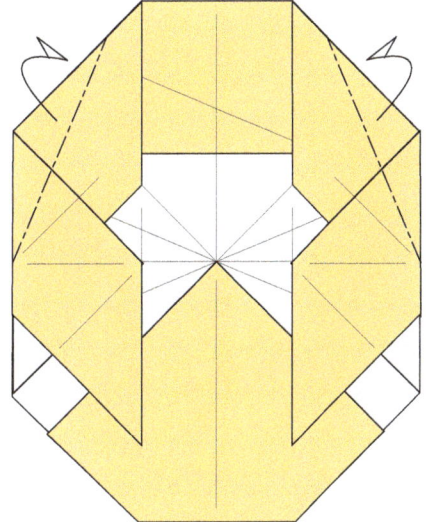

17. Mountain fold along the angle bisectors.

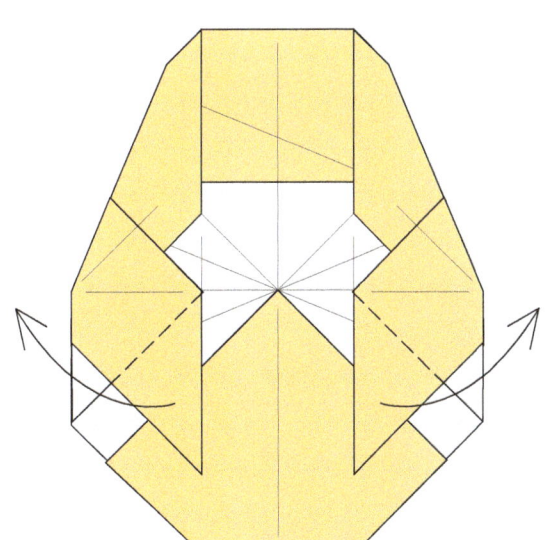

18. Valley fold the flaps outwards.

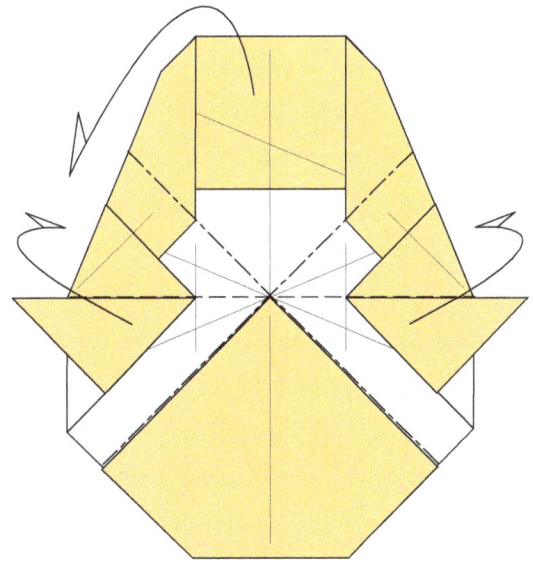

19. Fold the top section behind while reverse folding the sides.

angel

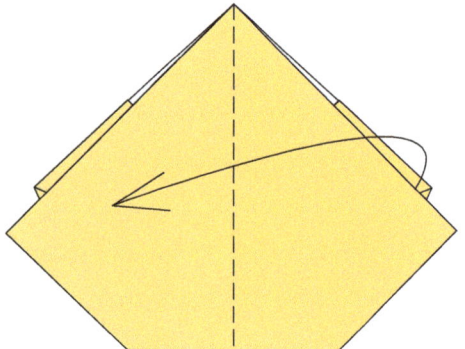

20. Swing over one flap.

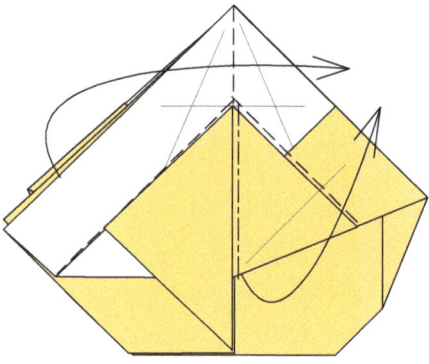

21. Swing the flap back while incorporating a reverse fold.

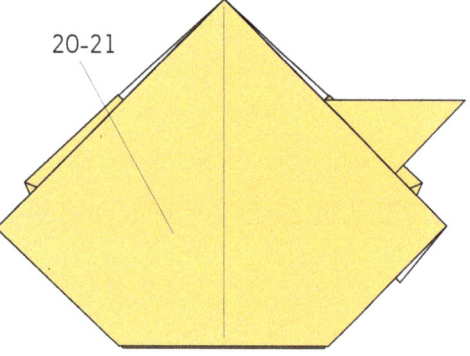

22. Repeat steps 20-21 in mirror image.

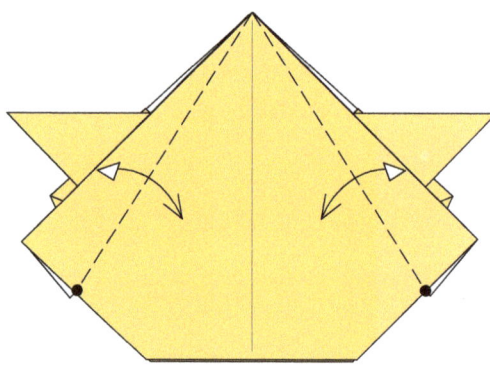

23. Precrease the top edges, noting the dotted corners.

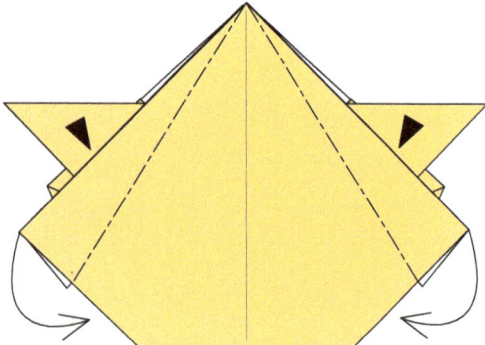

24. Reverse fold along the existing creases.

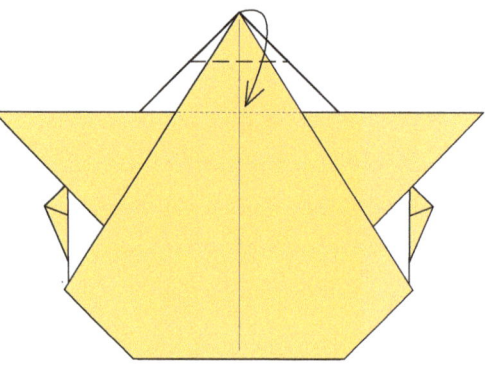

25. Valley fold to the imaginary line.

angel

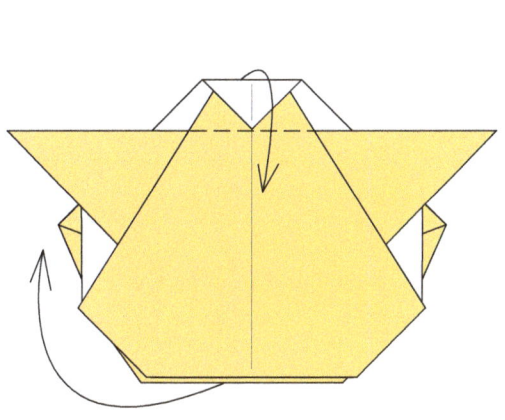

26. Valley fold the top edge down while swinging the back section up.

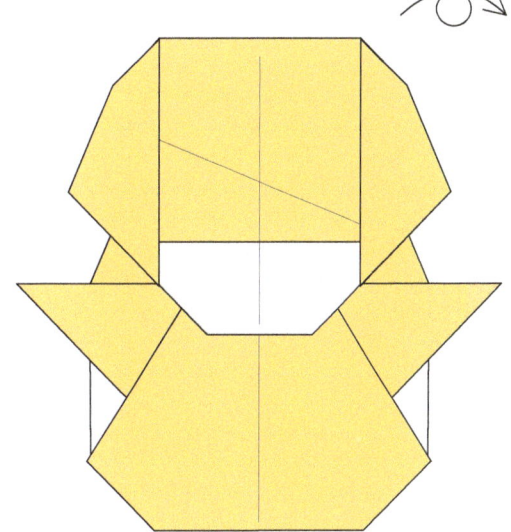

27. Turn over.

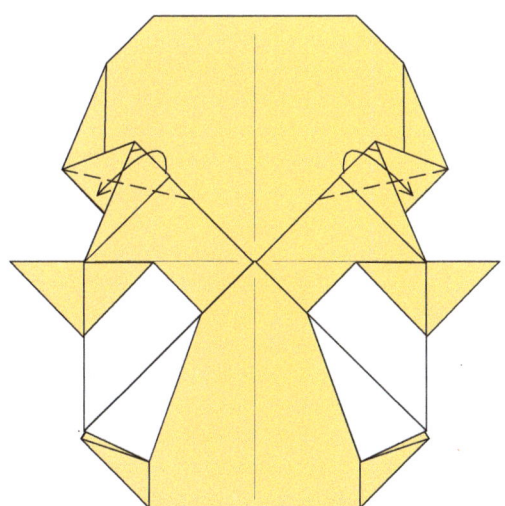

28. Valley fold the edges down.

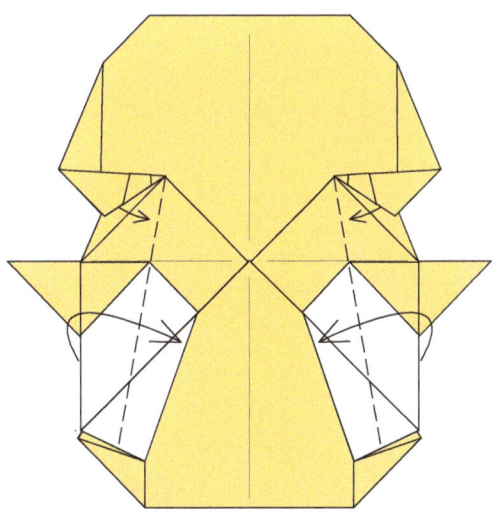

29. Valley fold the sides inward, pulling out the trapped paper.

angel

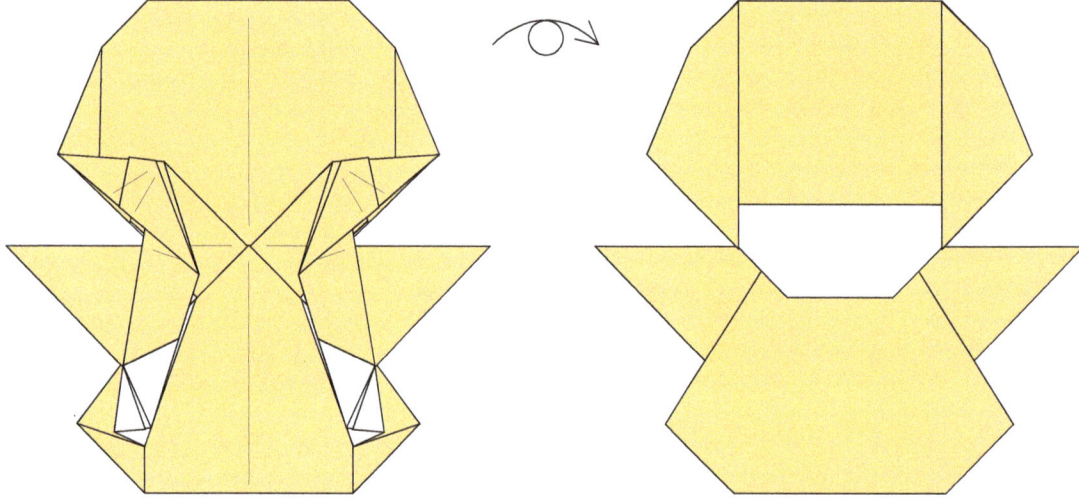

30. Turn over.

31. Completed *Angel*.

COWHAND

cowhand

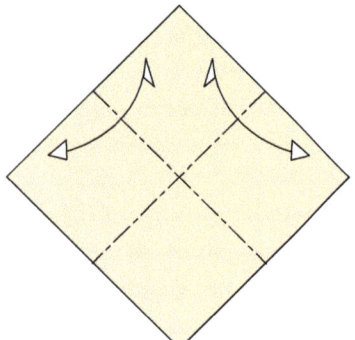

1. Precrease the sides in half with mountain folds.

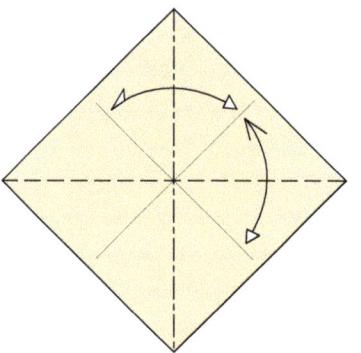

2. Precrease along the diagonals with a mountain fold and a valley fold.

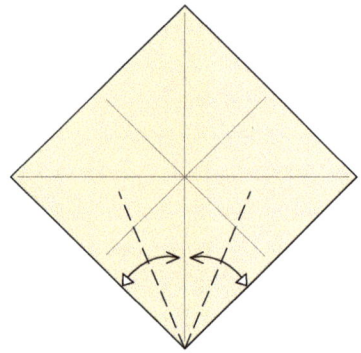

3. Precrease the bottom along the angle bisectors.

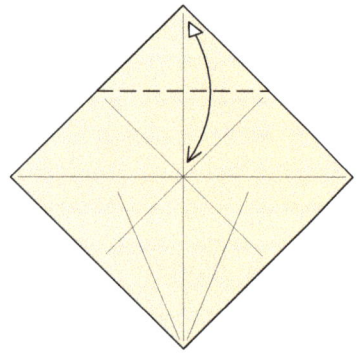

4. Precrease the top section in half.

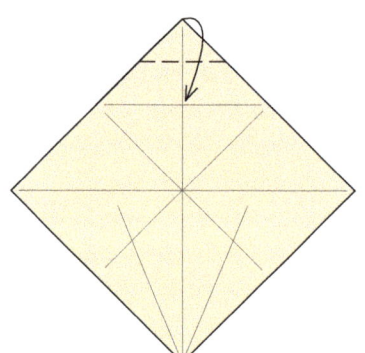

5. Valley fold to the last crease.

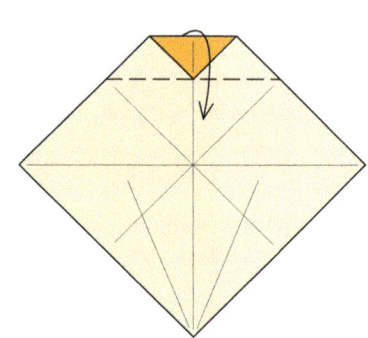

6. Valley fold along the existing crease.

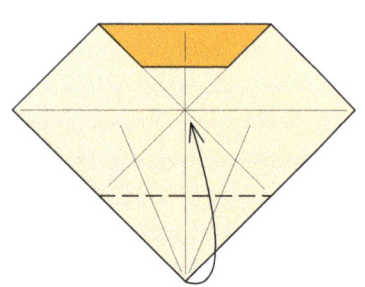

7. Valley fold to the intersection of creases.

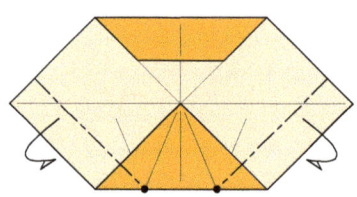

8. Mountain fold the sides starting from the dotted intersections.

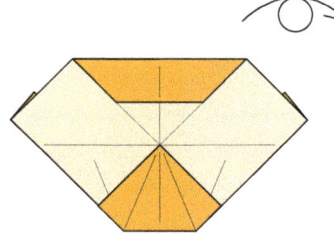

9. Turn over.

68

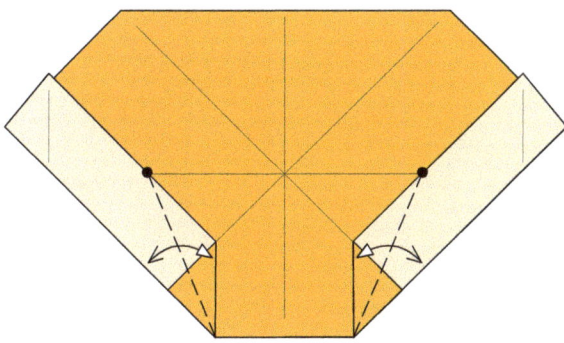

10. Precrease along the angle bisectors, noting the dotted intersections.

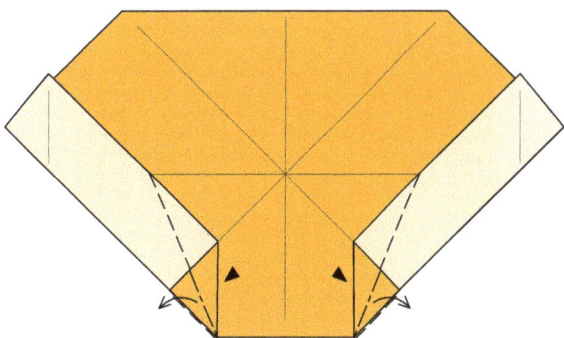

11. Squash fold along the existing creases.

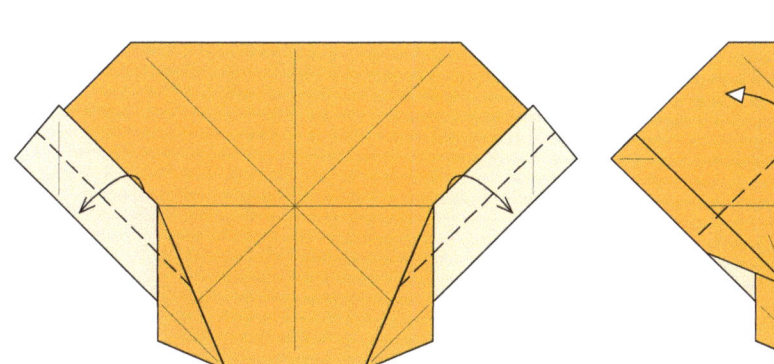

12. Valley fold the edges in half.

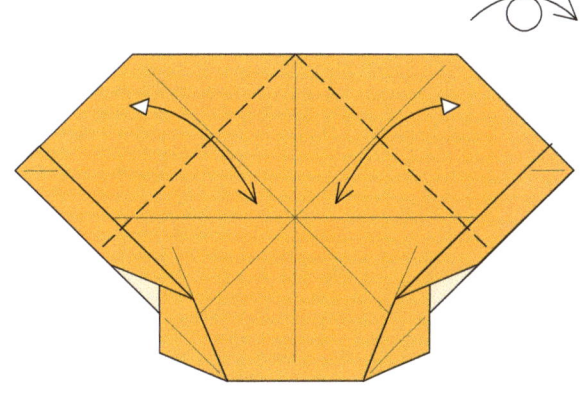

13. Precrease the sides in half. Turn over.

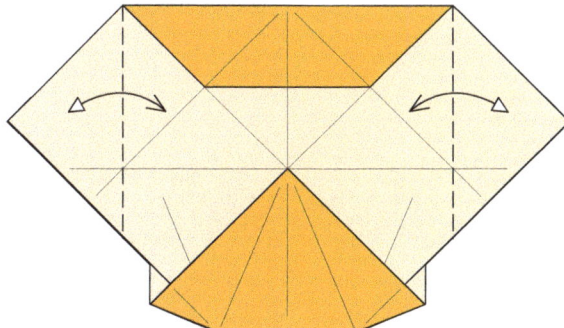

14. Precrease the sides.

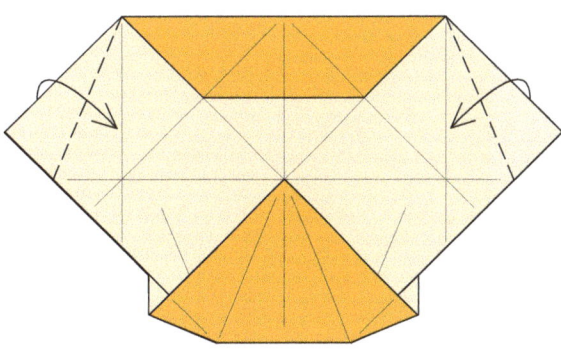

15. Valley fold to the previous creases.

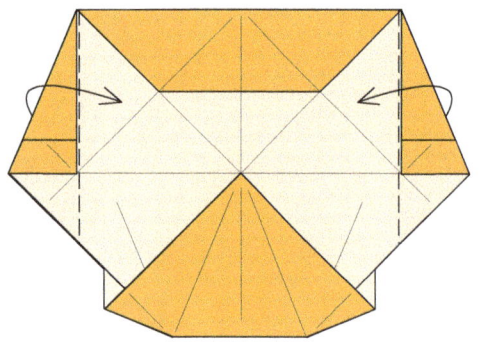

16. Valley fold along the existing creases.

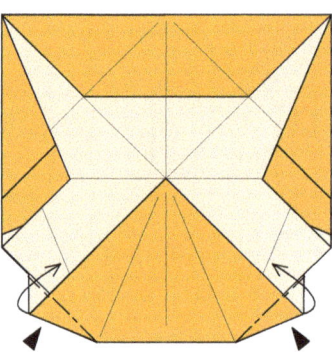

17. Reverse fold the corners in.

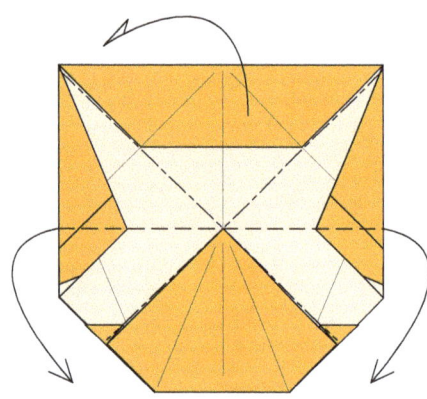

18. Fold the top section behind while reverse folding in the sides.

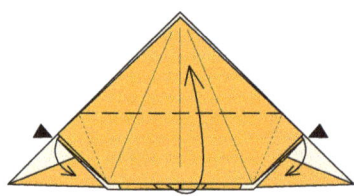

19. Lightly fold the bottom edge up, allowing the hidden corners to squash fold flat.

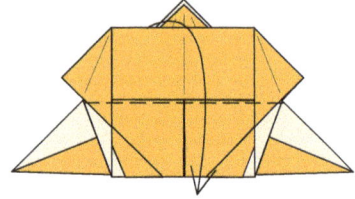

20. Swing the edge back down.

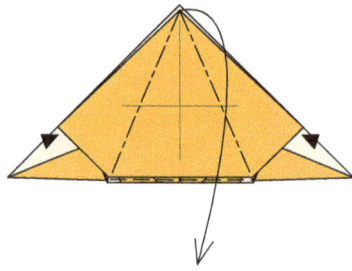

21. Bring the top single layer down, forming a petal fold.

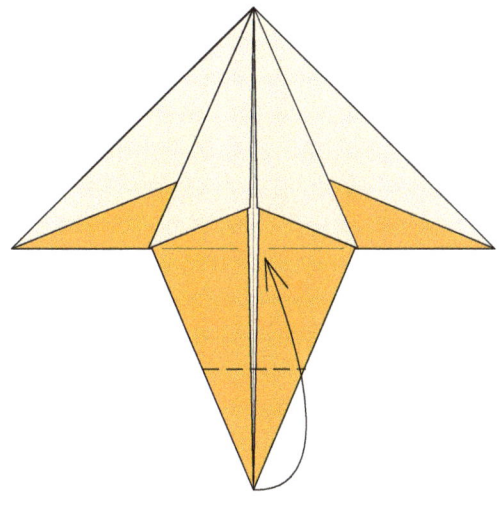
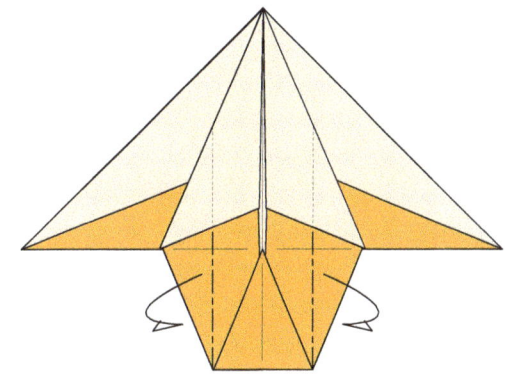

22. Valley fold to the center of the flap.

23. Mountain fold the sides to the center. Parts of the folds are hidden.

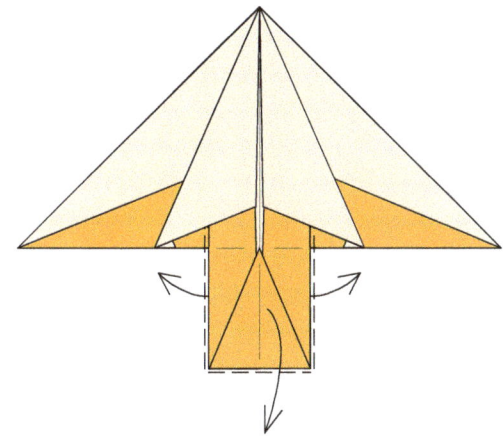
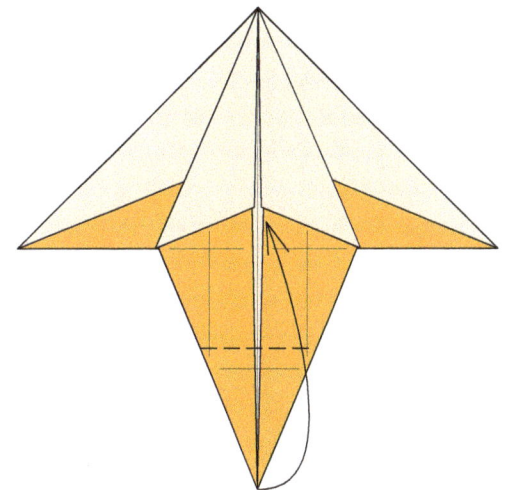

24. Open out the sides and the bottom flap.

25. Valley fold to the intersection of folded edges.

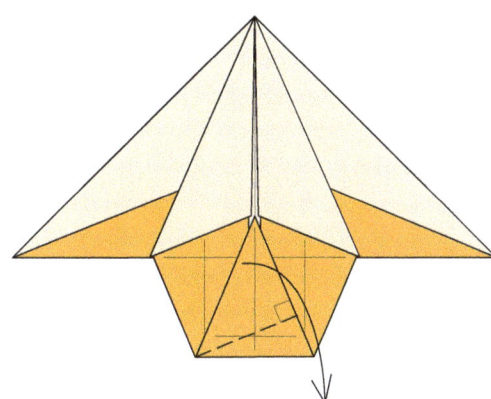
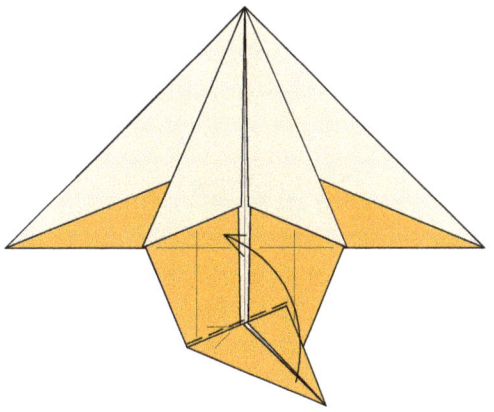

26. Valley fold the flap over, keeping the side edges aligned.

27. Swing the flap back up.

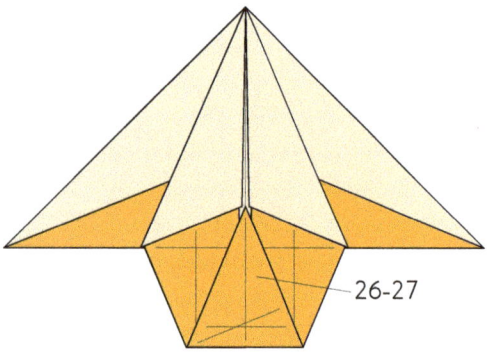

28. Repeat steps 26-27 in mirror image.

29. Swing the flap down.

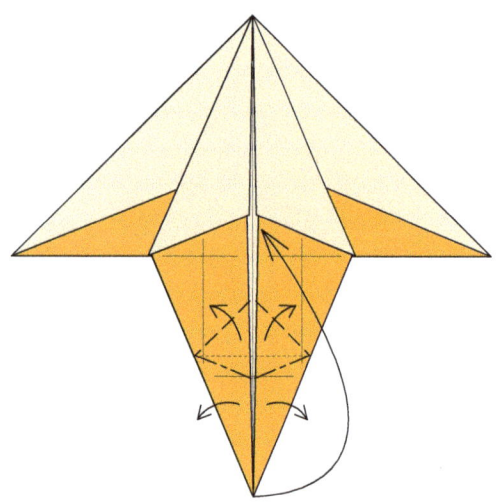

30. Spread apart the top layers while folding the flap up.

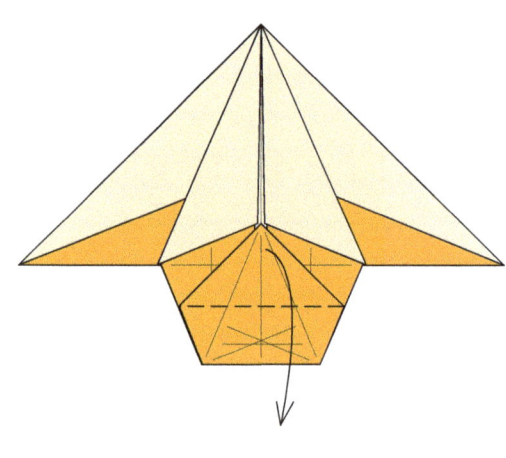

31. Valley fold the top layer down.

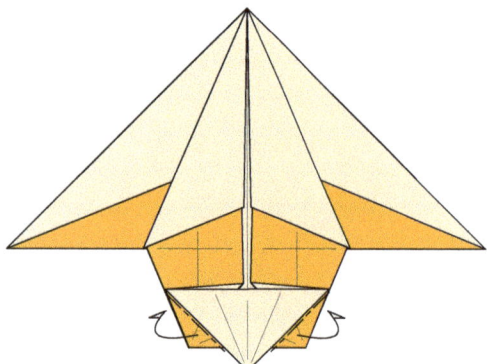

32. Mountain fold the corners behind.

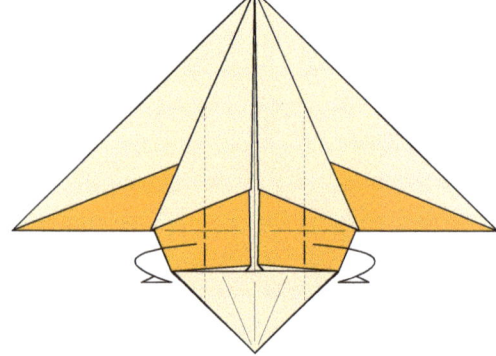

33. Mountain fold the sides along the existing creases.

cowhand

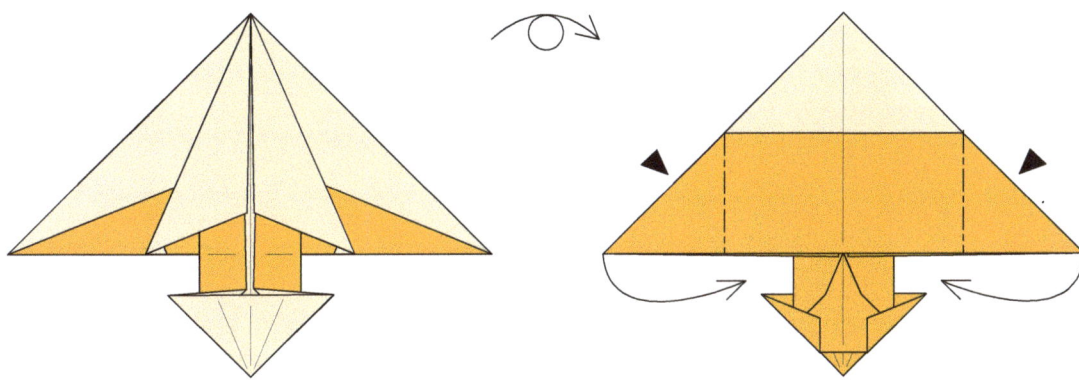

34. Turn over.

35. Reverse fold the side corners.

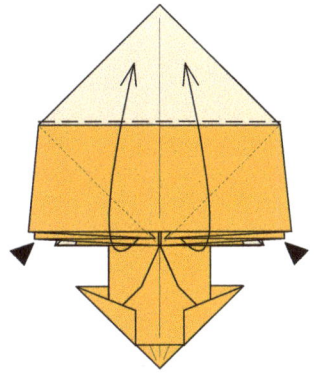

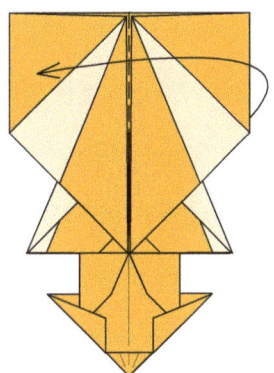

36. Bring the top set of layers up, allowing the bottom hidden corners to squash fold flat.

37. Swing over one flap.

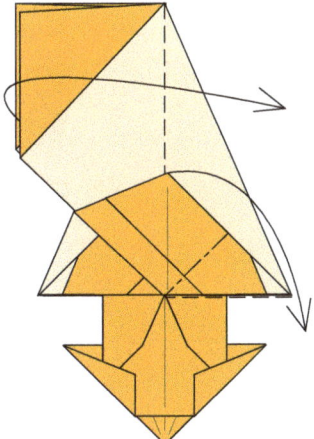

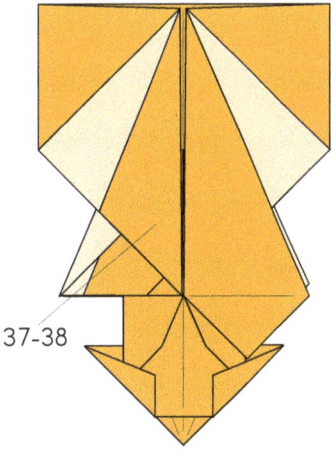

38. Swing the flap back while pulling out the bottom edge.

39. Repeat steps 37-38 in mirror image.

cowhand

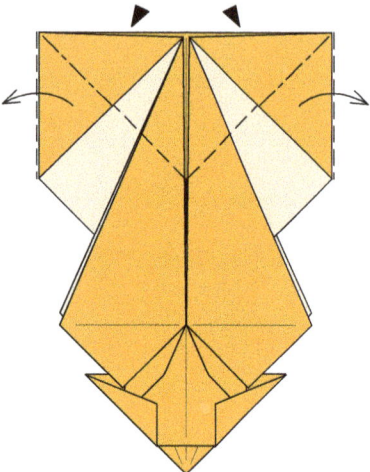

40. Squash fold the top layers.

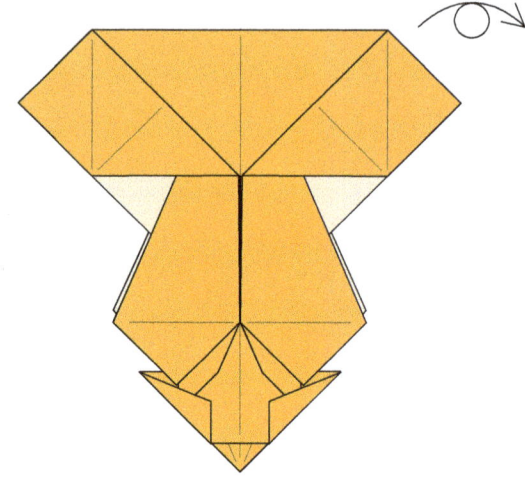

41. Turn over.

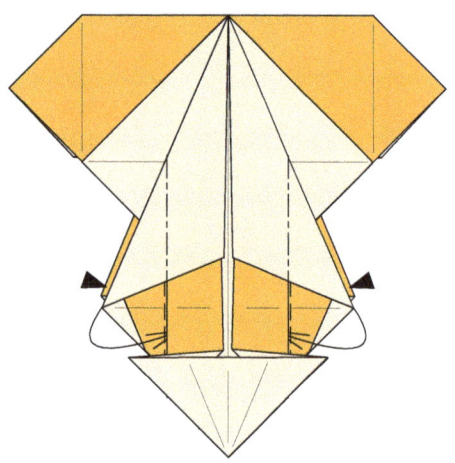

42. Reverse fold the sides.

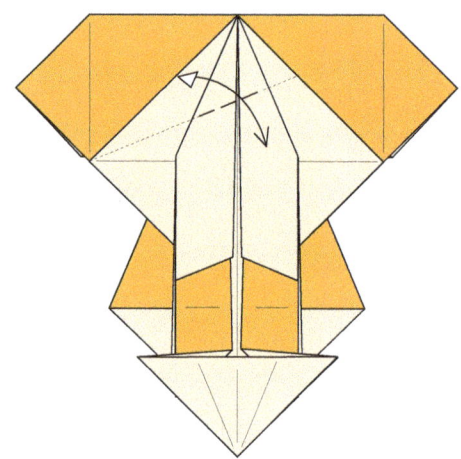

43. Precrease the top flap partway along the angle bisector.

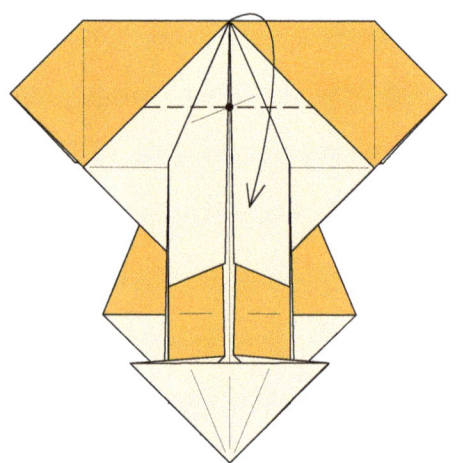

44. Valley fold through the dotted intersection.

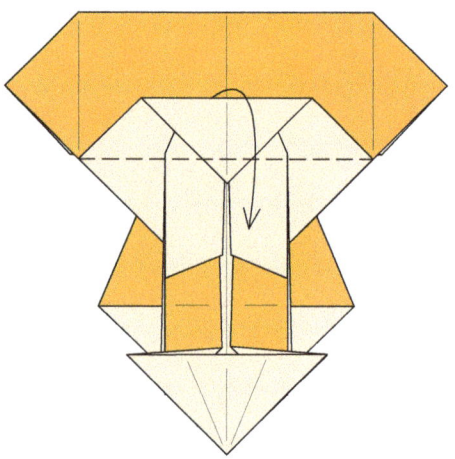

45. Valley fold the flap down.

cowhand

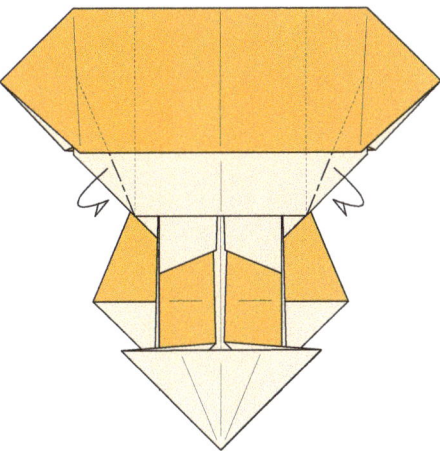

46. Mountain fold the corners along the (imaginary) angle bisectors.

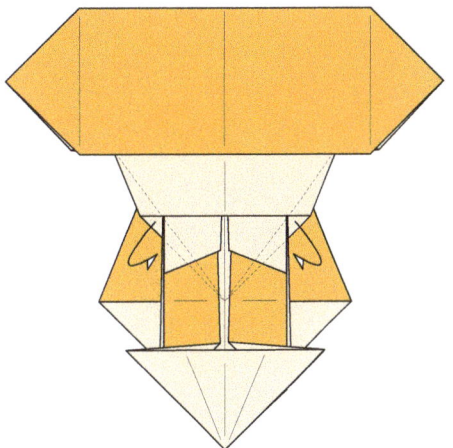

47. Mountain fold the trapped edge inside.

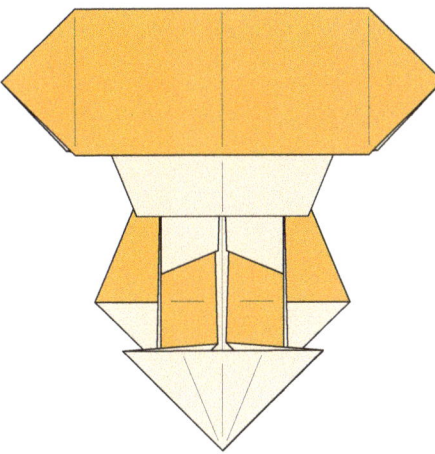

48. Turn over.

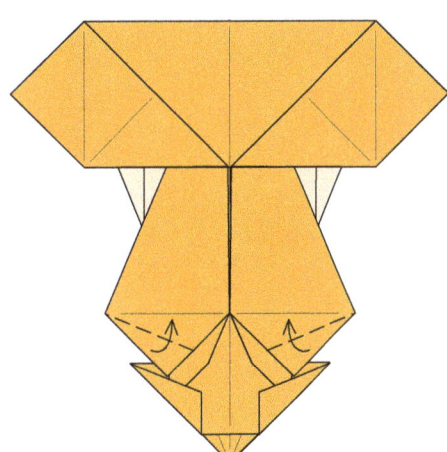

49. Valley fold along the angle bisectors.

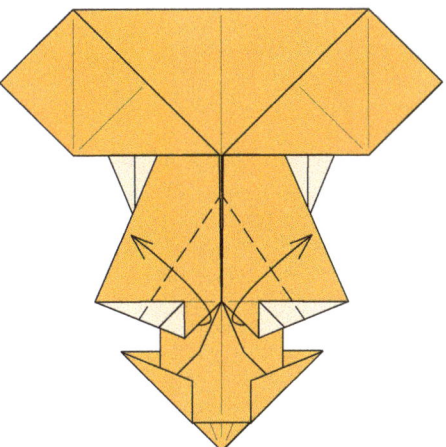

50. Valley fold the short edges to meet the outer edges.

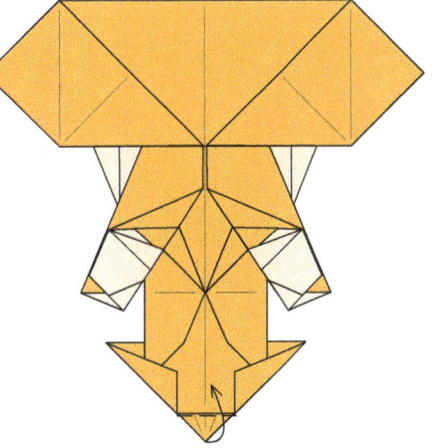

51. Valley fold the corner up.

75

cowhand

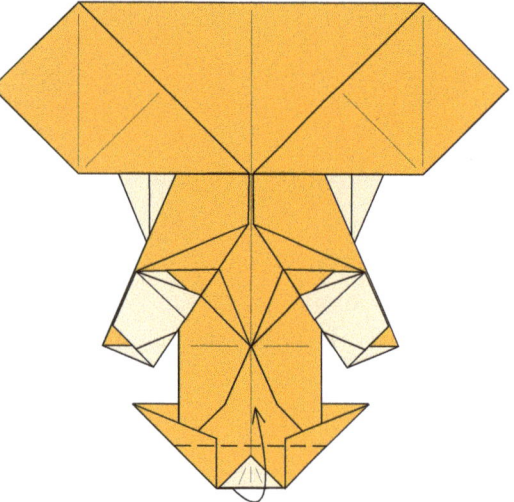

52. Valley fold the bottom section in half.

53. Valley fold the bottom section up.

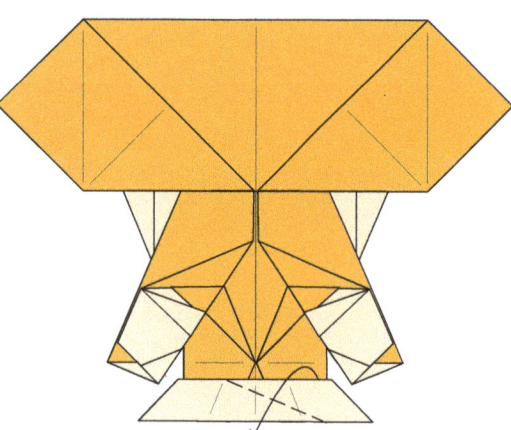

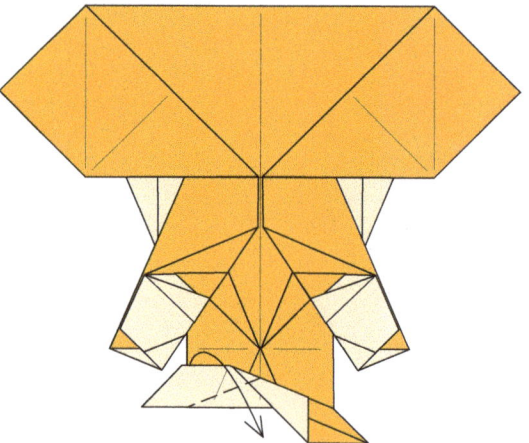

54. Fold the flap down do the bottom edge lies straight.

55. Valley fold the other side over to match.

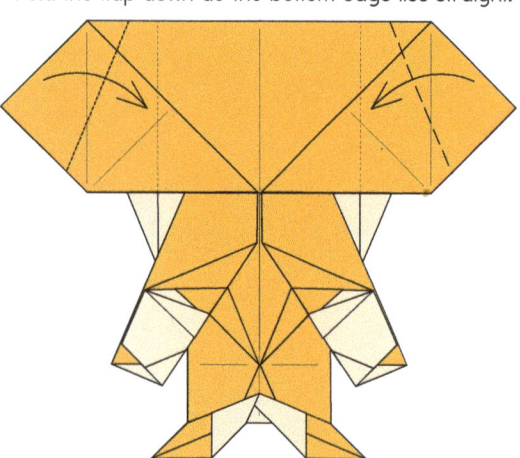

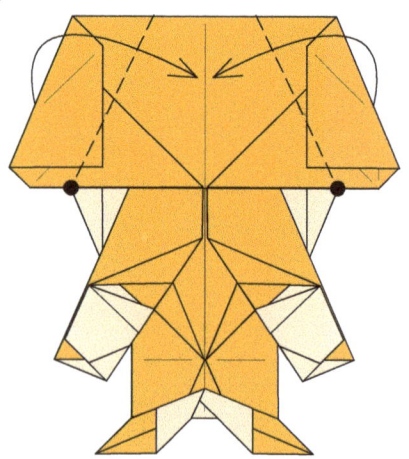

56. Valley fold the sides to meet the imaginary lines.

57. Valley fold the corners to the center, starting from the dotted corners.

cowhand

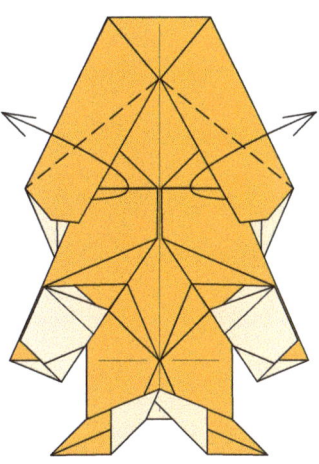

58. Valley fold the top flaps outwards from corner to corner.

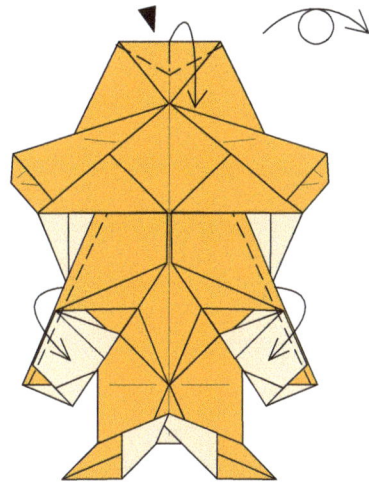

59. Push in the top edge, shaping the hat as desired. Round the edges of the arms slightly. Turn over.

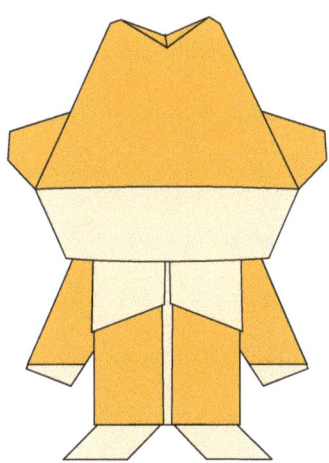

60. Completed *Cowhand*.

TEDDY BEAR

teddy bear

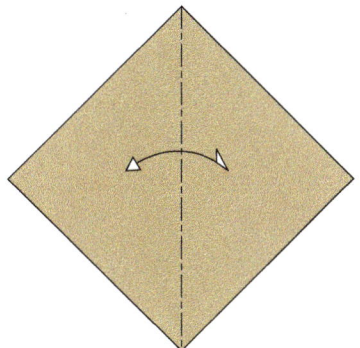

1. Precrease along the diagonal with a mountain fold.

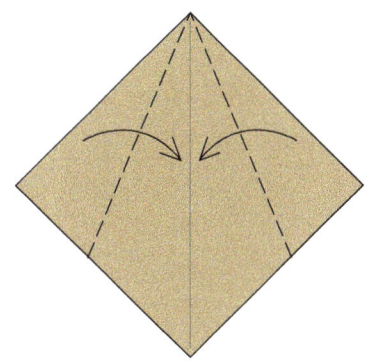

2. Valley fold the sides to the center.

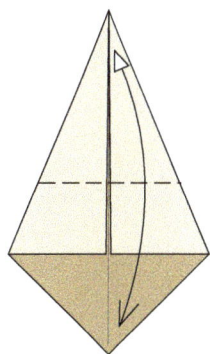

3. Precrease in half.

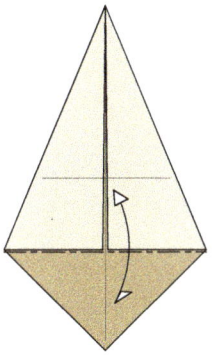

4. Precrease with a mountain fold.

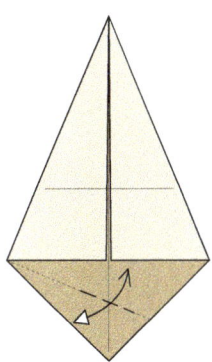

5. Precrease partway along the angle bisector.

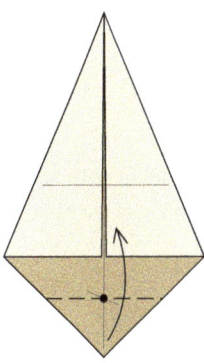

6. Valley fold through the dotted intersection of creases.

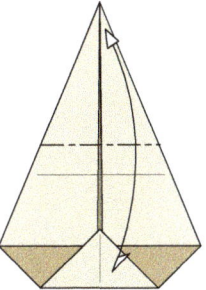

7. Precrease in half with a mountain fold.

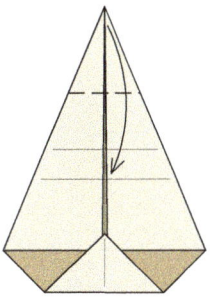

8. Valley fold to the lower crease.

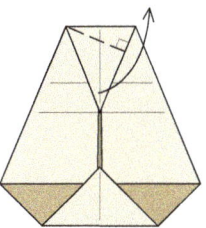

9. Valley fold up, keeping the edges aligned.

79

teddy bear

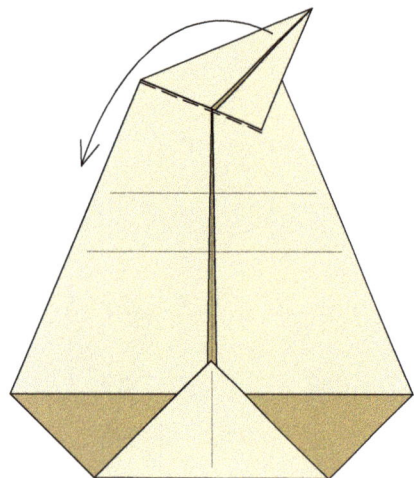

10. Unfold the last step.

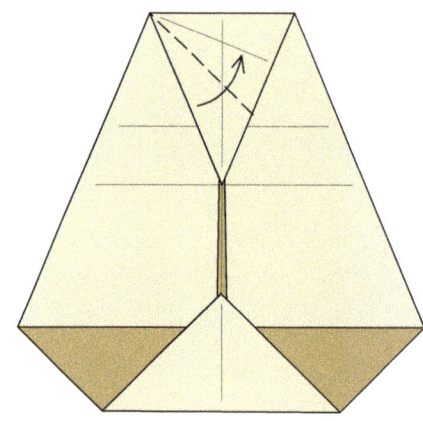

11. Valley fold towards the crease.

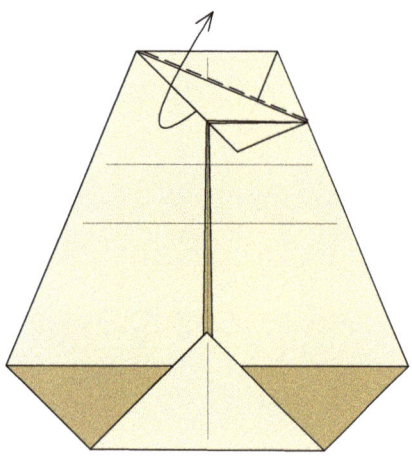

12. Pull around a single layer and flatten.

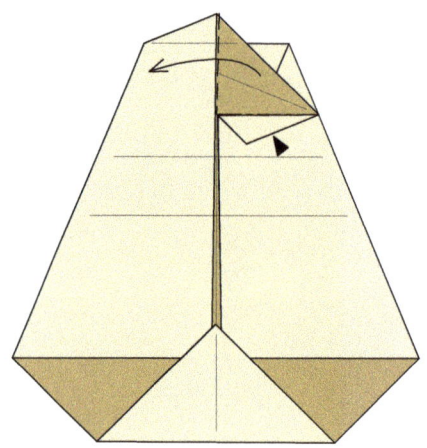

13. Squash fold the center flap over.

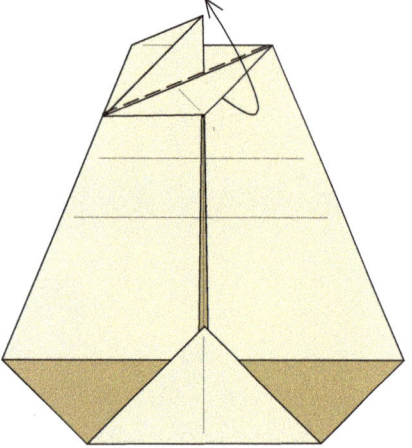

14. Pull around a single layer and flatten.

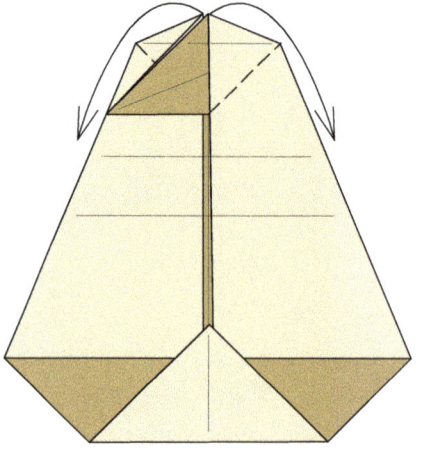

15. Spread open the top flaps and flatten.

teddy bear

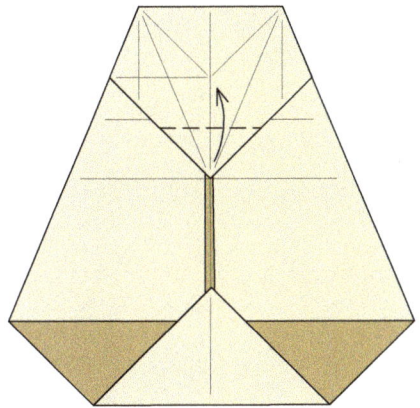

16. Lightly valley fold to the intersections of creases.

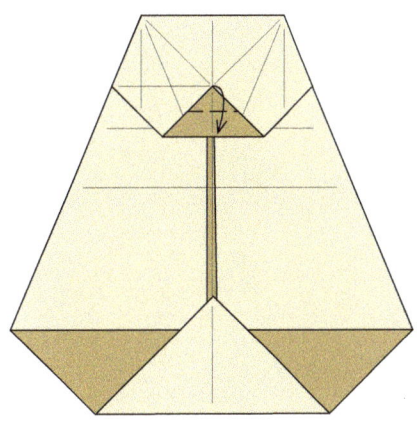

17. Lightly valley fold the corner down.

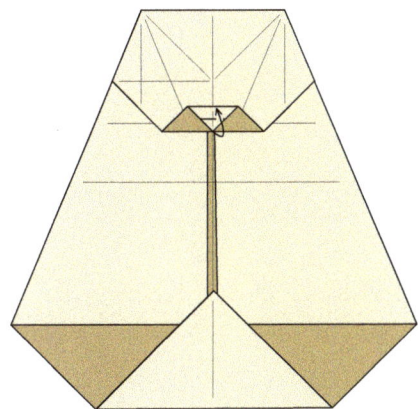

18. Valley fold the corner up.

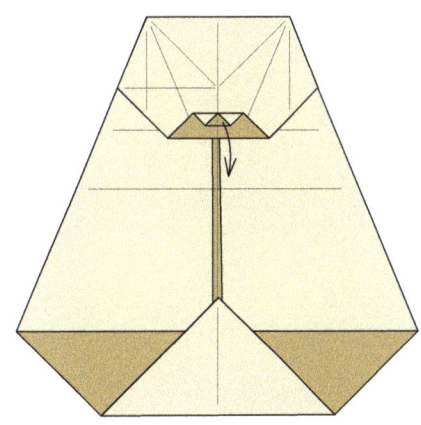

19. Unfold the pleat, leaving the last fold in place.

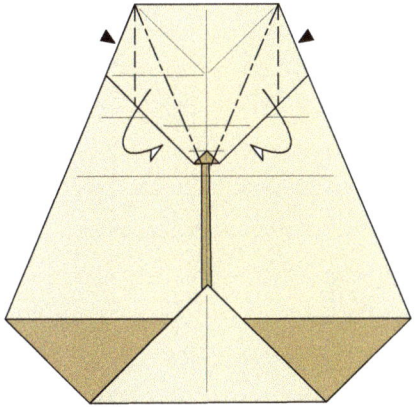

20. Reverse fold the sides.

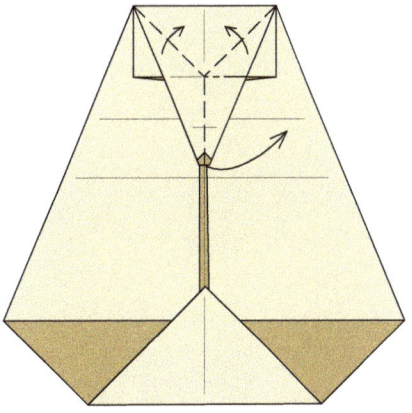

21. Rabbit ear the flap over.

81

teddy bear

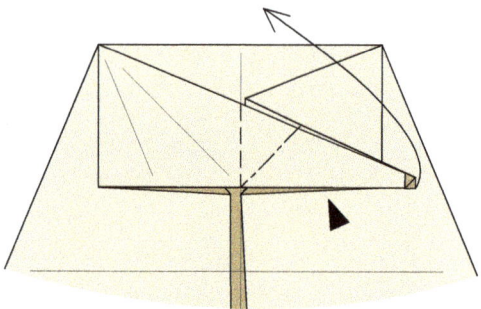

22. Squash fold the flap up.

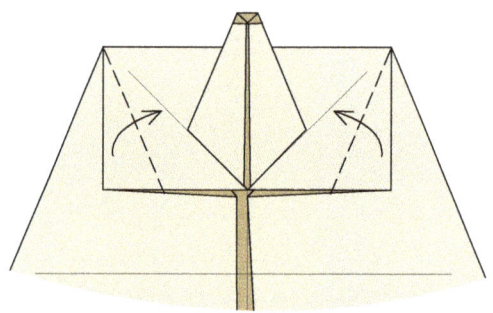

23. Valley fold the edges towards the creases.

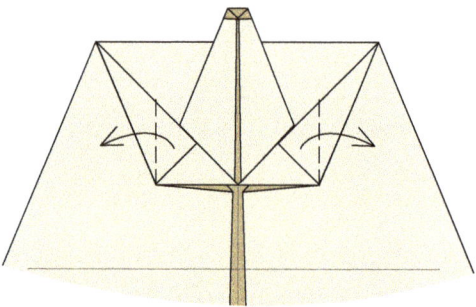

24. Valley fold the corners outwards.

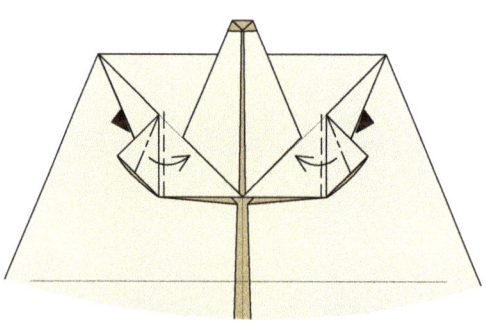

25. Squash fold the flaps.

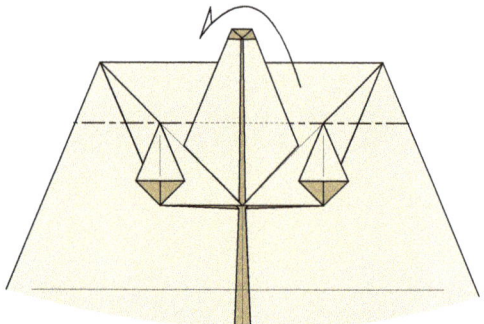

26. Mountain fold the edge behind.

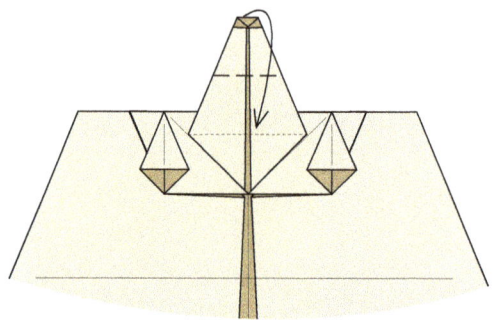

27. Valley fold to the imaginary intersection.

teddy bear

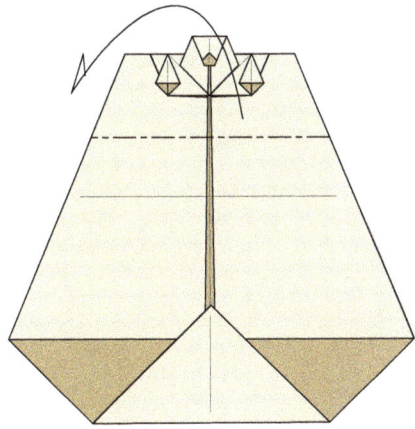

28. Mountain fold behind along the existing crease.

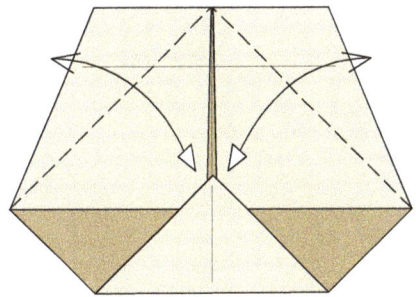

29. Precrease the top layers.

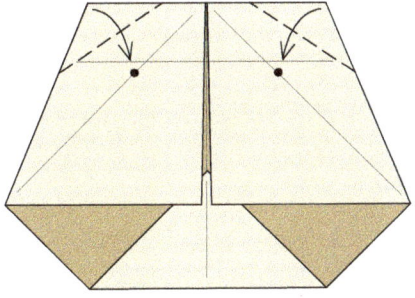

30. Valley fold the corners to the creases, keeping the bottom edges straight.

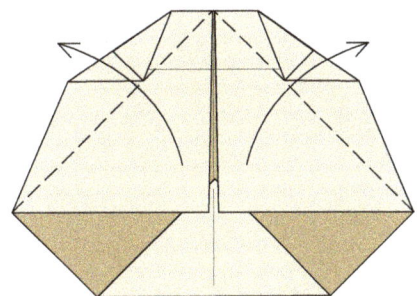

31. Valley fold the top layers outwards.

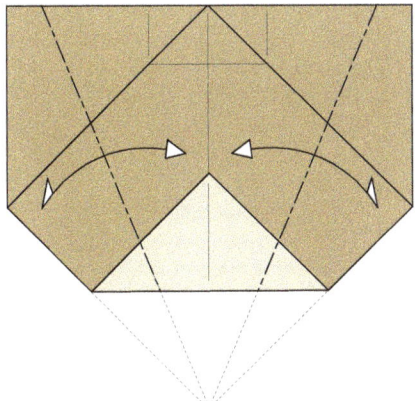

32. Precrease along the imaginary angle bisectors with mountain folds.

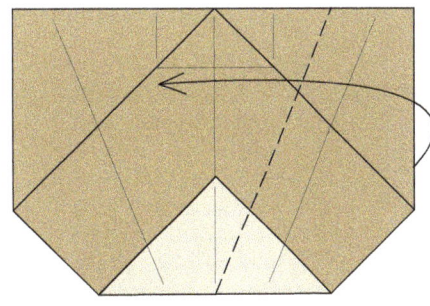

33. Valley fold to the inner folded edge.

teddy bear

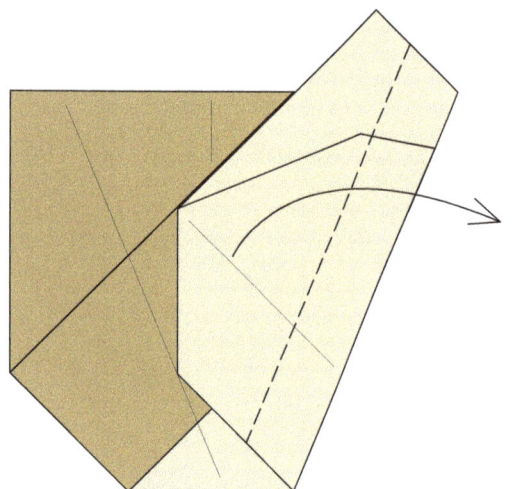

34. Valley fold along the existing crease.

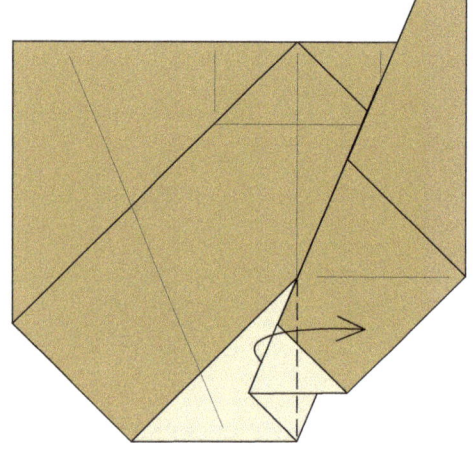

35. Valley fold along the center.

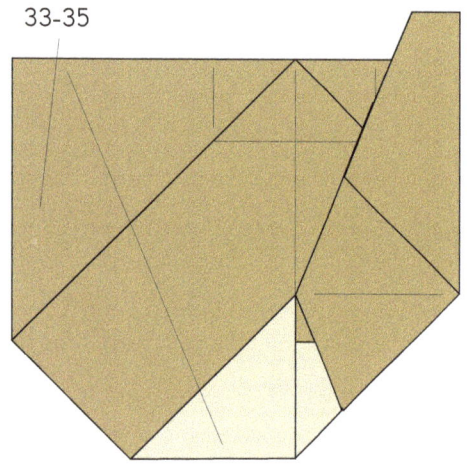

36. Repeat steps 33-35 in mirror image.

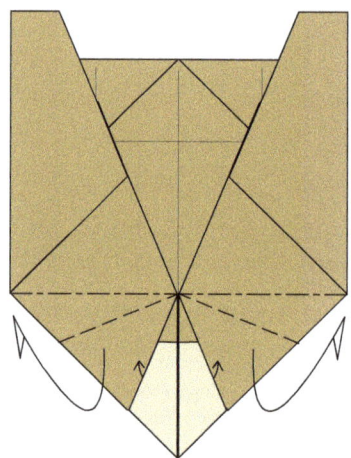

37. Pull out the bottom pleats and swivel fold behind.

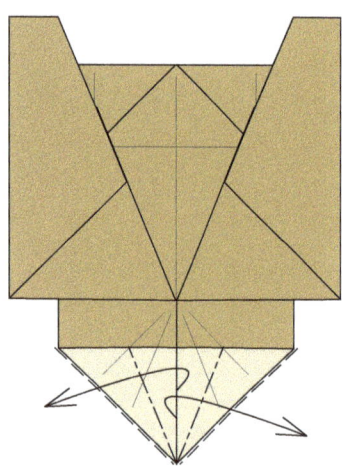

38. Pull out the trapped layers and flatten.

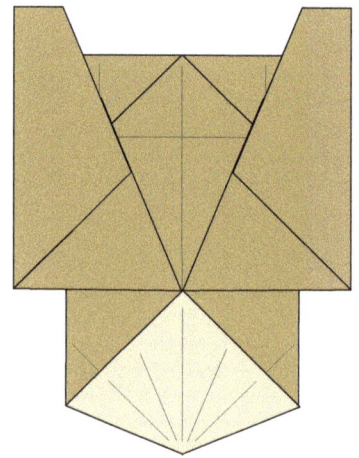

39. Turn over.

teddy bear

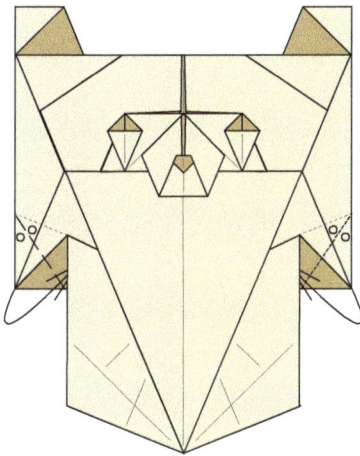

40. Tuck the corners in along the indicated (imaginary) angle bisectors.

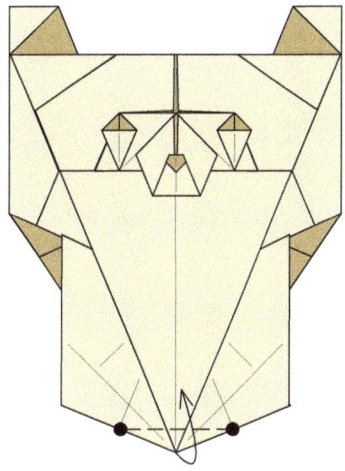

41. Valley fold the corner up between the dotted intersections.

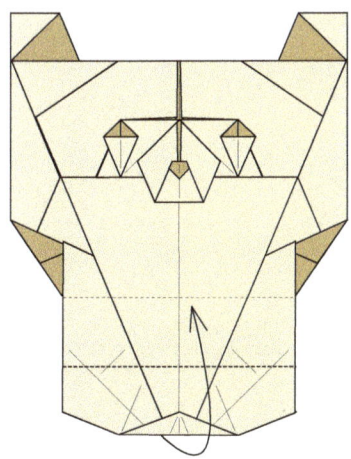

42. Valley fold to the imaginary line.

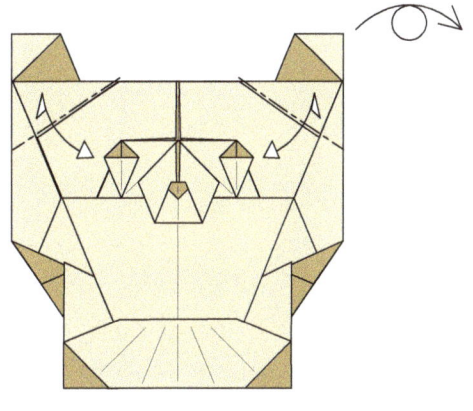

43. Precrease the top flaps with mountain folds. Turn over.

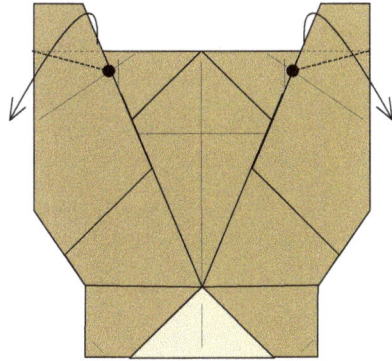

44. Valley fold the top flaps outwards using the dotted intersections.

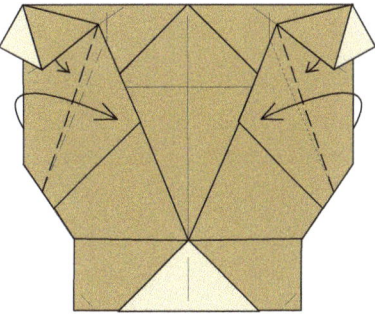

45. Valley fold the side edges through and flatten.

teddy bear

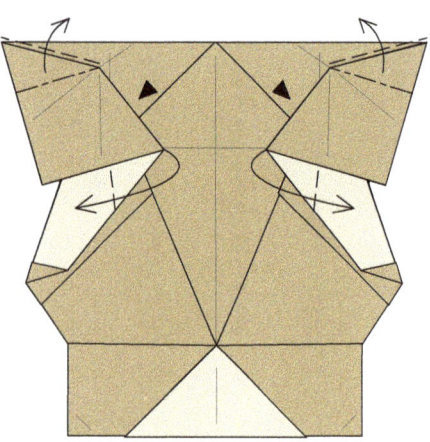

46. Swivel fold the top layers up so the top edges are aligned.

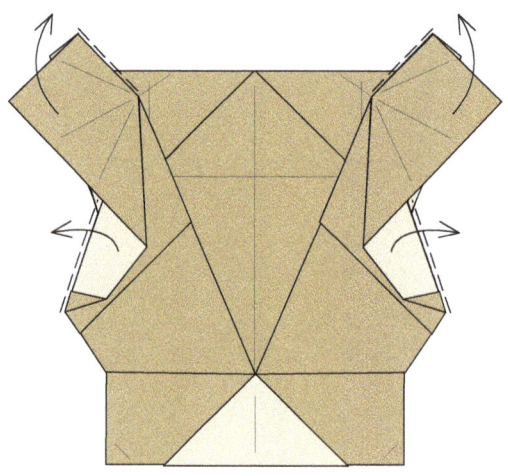

47. Open out the pleated sections.

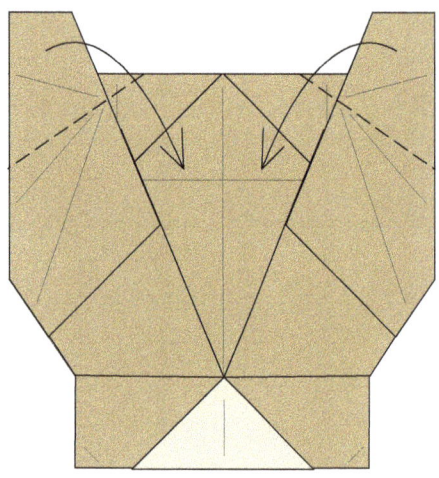

48. Valley fold the flaps along the existing creases.

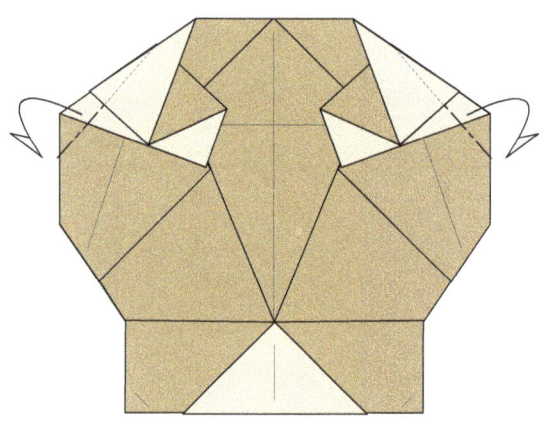

49. Mountain fold the edges along the existing creases.

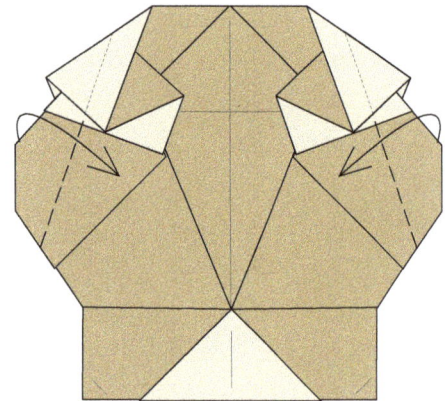

50. Valley fold the sides along the existing creases.

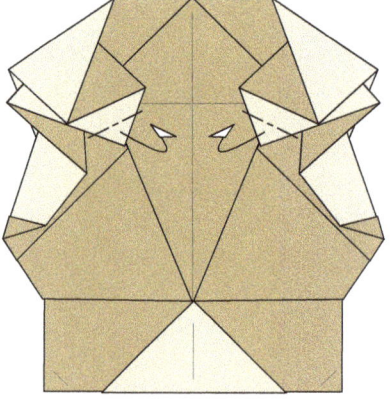

51. Mountain fold the corners.

teddy bear

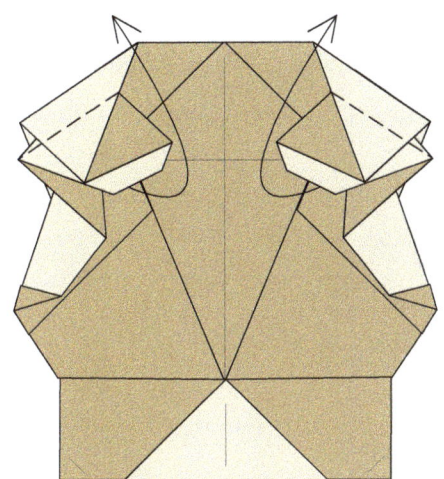

52. Valley fold the flaps straight up.

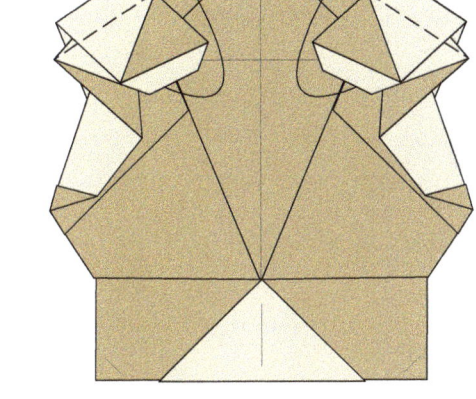

53. Turn over.

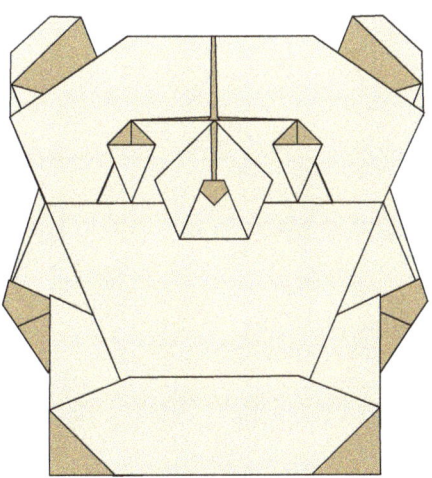

54. Completed *Teddy Bear*.

87

WITCH

witch

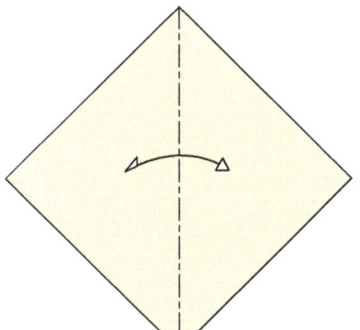

1. Precrease along the diagonal with a mountain fold.

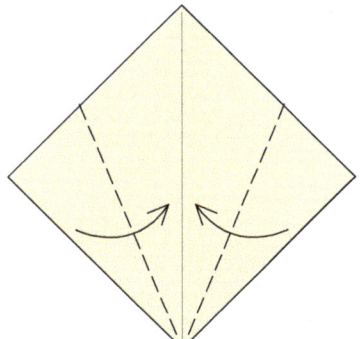

2. Valley fold to the center.

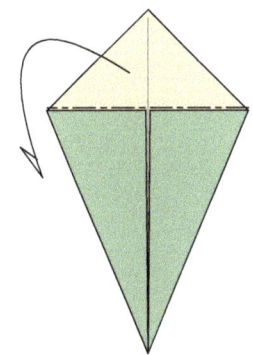

3. Mountain fold the top corner behind.

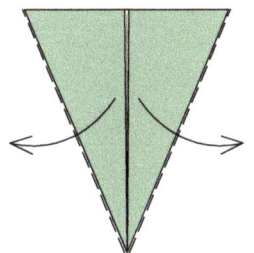

4. Open out the side flaps.

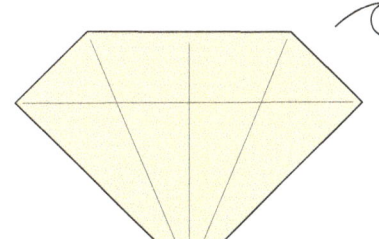

5. Turn over.

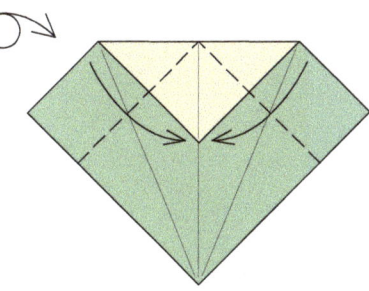

6. Valley fold the sides to the center.

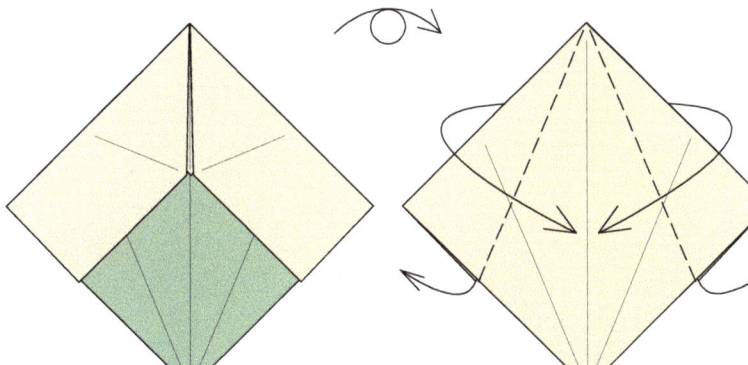

7. Turn over.

8. Valley fold the sides to the center, allowing the flaps from behind to swing forward.

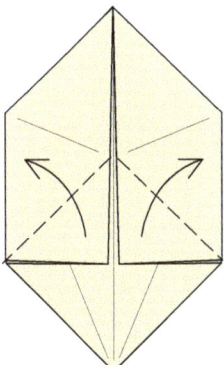

9. Valley fold the top flaps to the outer edges.

89

witch

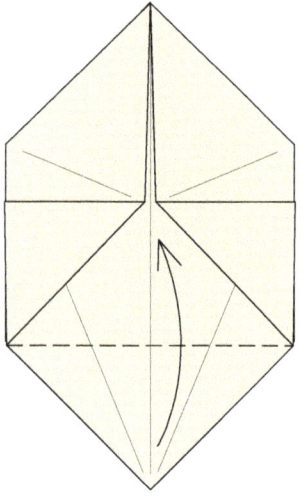

10. Valley fold the corner up.

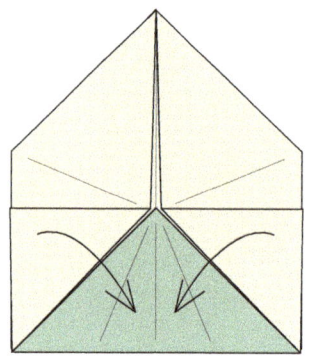

11. Swing the flaps back down.

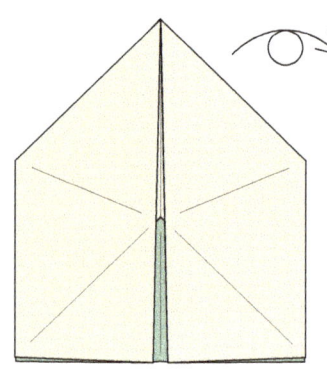

12. Turn over.

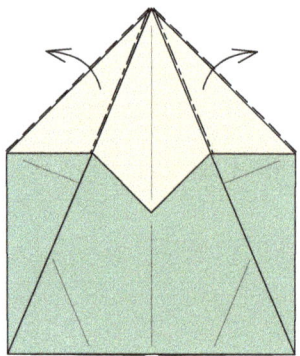

13. Slide the trapped layers outwards and squash fold flat.

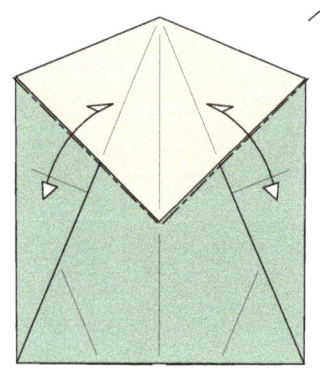

14. Precrease along the edges with mountain folds. Turn over.

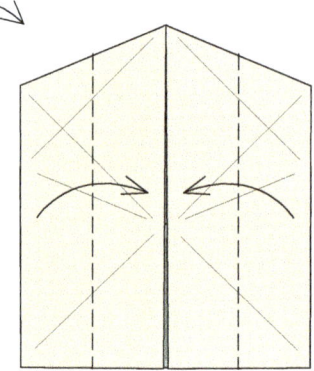

15. Valley fold the sides to the center.

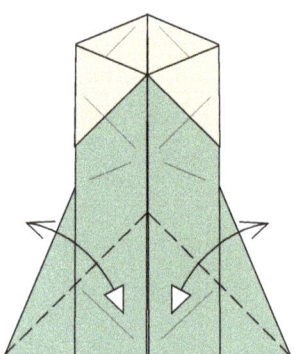

16. Precrease the top layers.

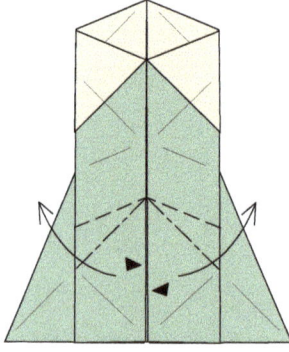

17. Pleat the top layers up, allowing squash folds to form at the bottom.

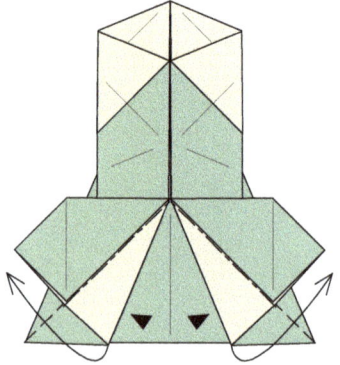

18. Reverse fold the corners.

witch

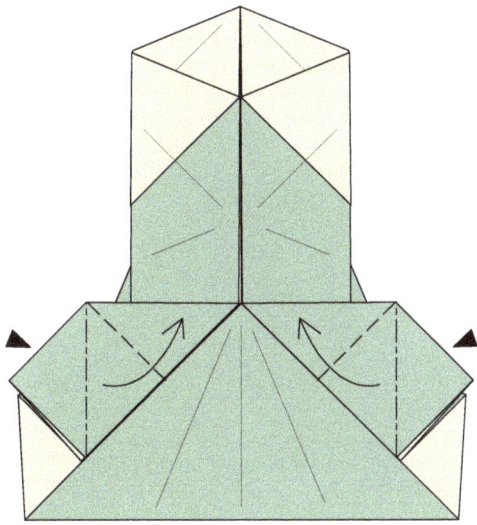

19. Squash fold the corners over at each side.

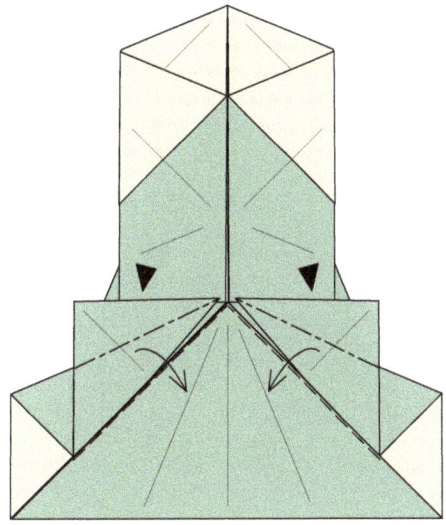

20. Lightly squash fold the clusters of flaps down.

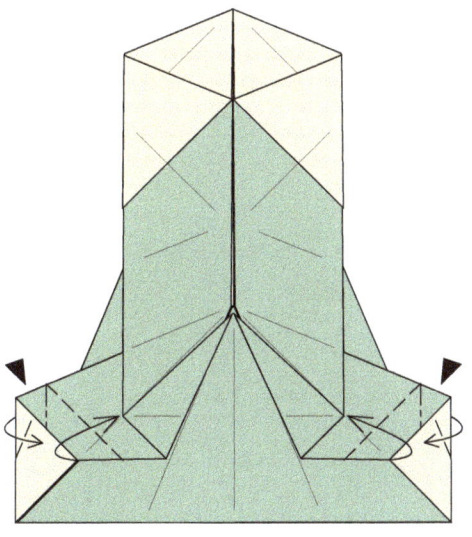

21. Valley fold the bottom corners over, allowing squash folds to form at the outer edges.

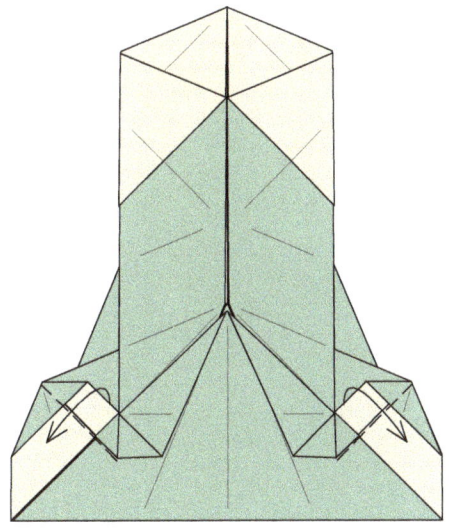

22. Swing the edges down.

91

witch

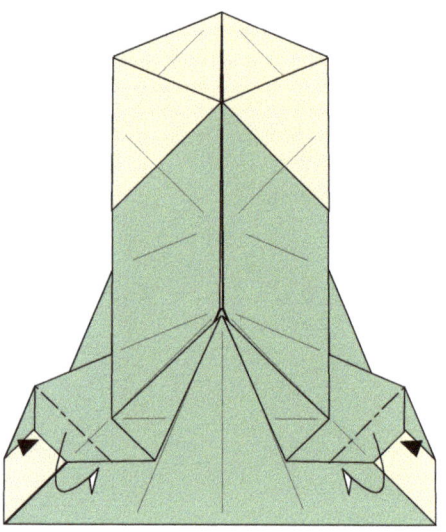

23. Reverse fold the edges in.

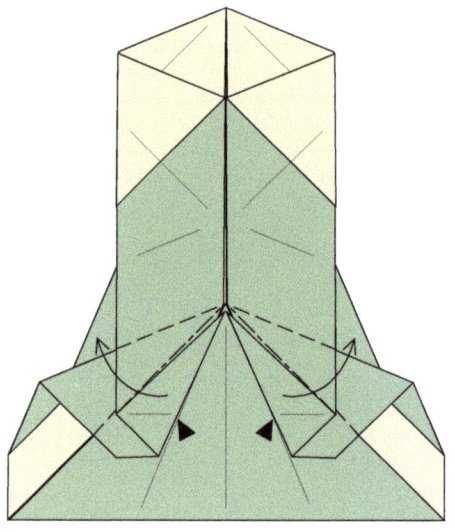

24. Squash fold the clusters up flaps back up.

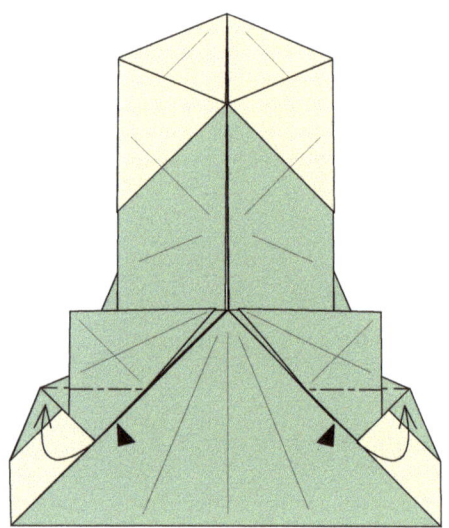

25. Reverse fold the side corners.

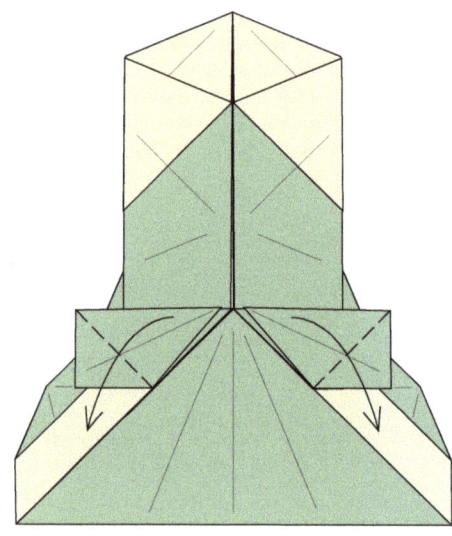

26. Swing down the top flaps.

witch

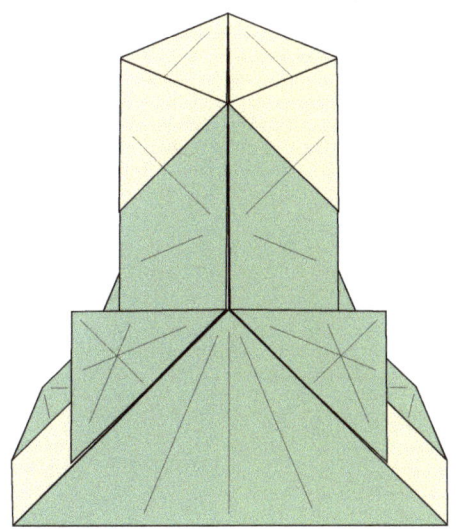

27. Turn over.

28. Valley fold the side over, passing through the hidden dotted intersection. A squash fold will form in the process.

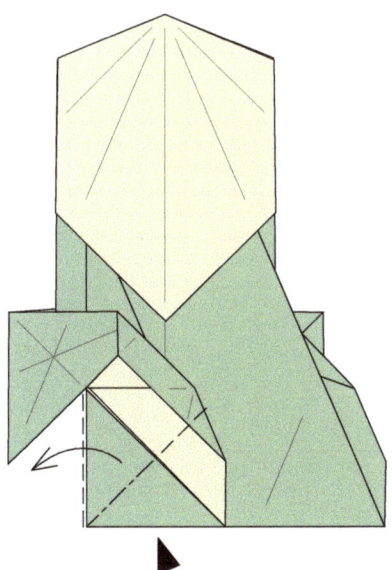

29. Squash fold the top layer over.

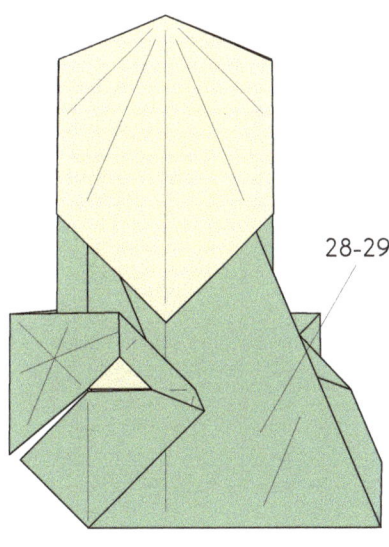

28-29

30. Repeat steps 28-29 in mirror image.

witch

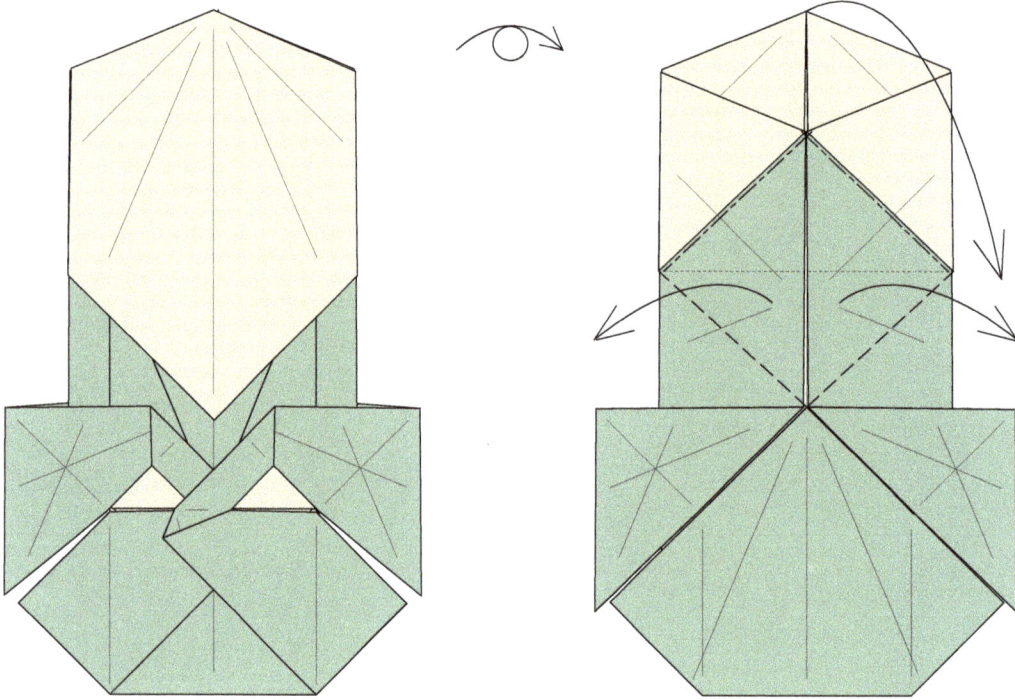

31. Turn over.

32. Swing the sides outwards, while folding the top down along the hidden crease line.

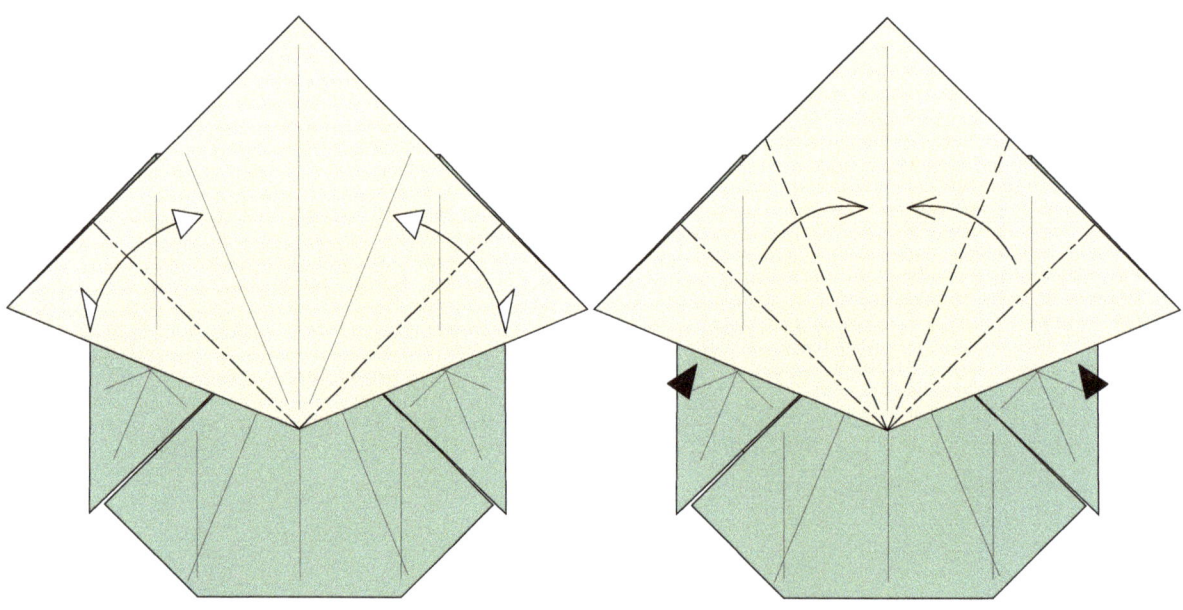

33. Precrease the sides with mountain folds.

34. Squash fold the sides.

witch

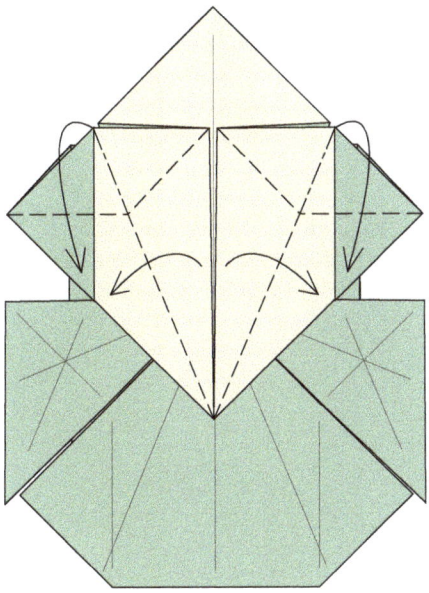

35. Fold the inner edges outwards while incorporating a reverse fold at each side.

36. Valley fold the sides to the center.

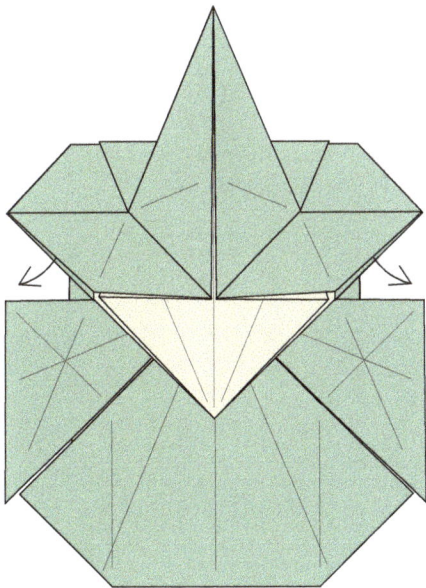

37. Pull out the trapped corners.

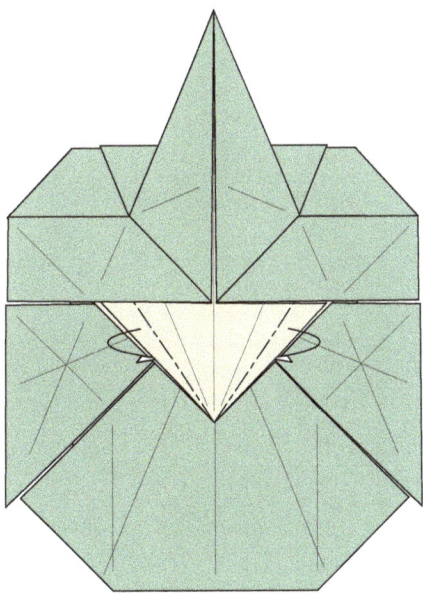

38. Mountain fold the edges along the angle bisectors.

witch

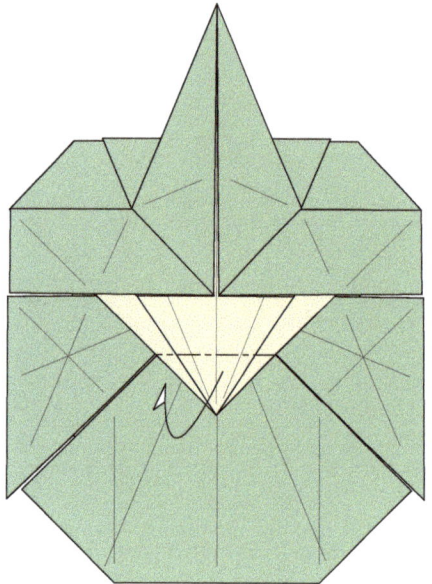

39. Mountain fold the corner in halfway.

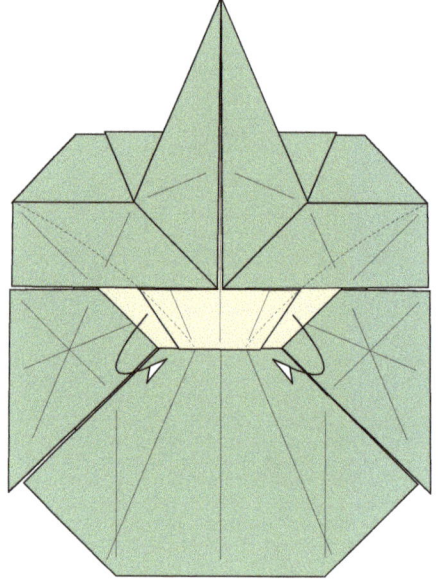

40. Mountain fold the side edges inside. These folds will slightly curve to facilitate this.

41. Turn over.

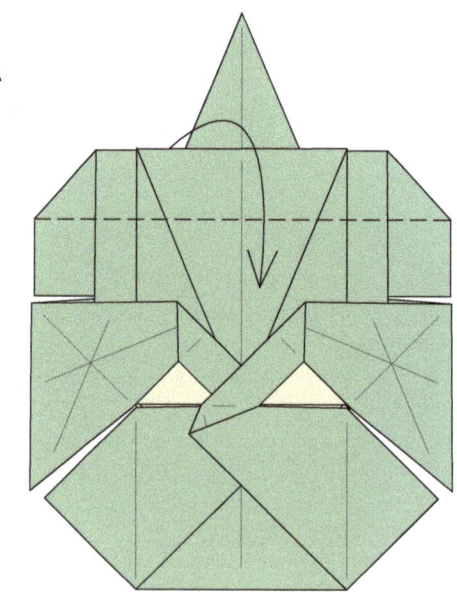

42. Valley fold the edge down.

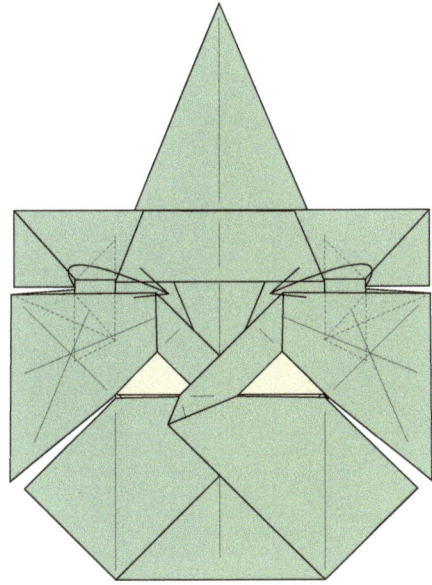

43. Swivel fold the (mostly) hidden side edges.

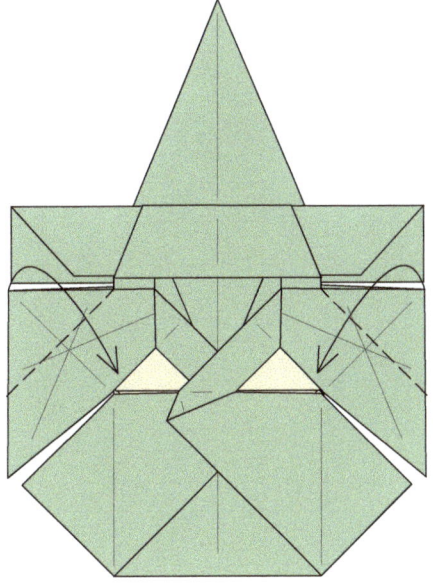

44. Valley fold the corners down.

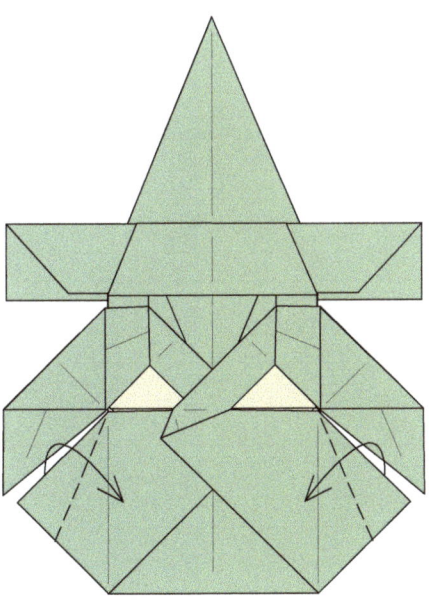

45. Valley fold along the angle bisectors.

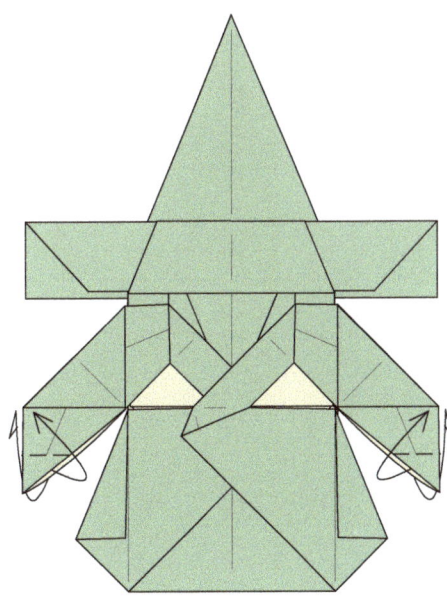

46. Outside reverse fold the corners.

witch

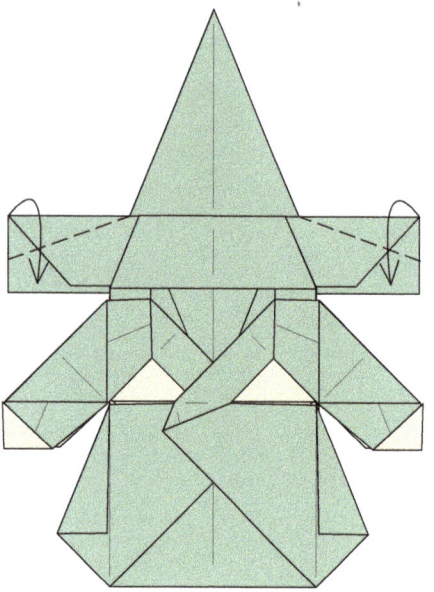

47. Valley fold the corners to the edge.

48. Turn over.

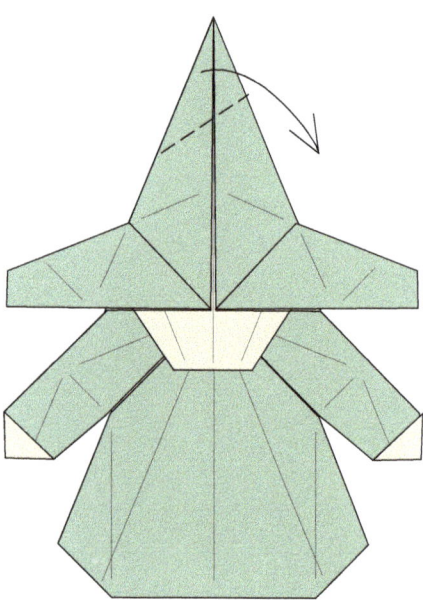

49. Valley fold the tip of the flap.

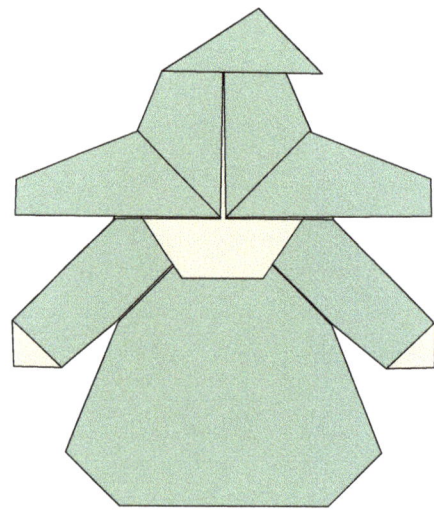

50. Completed *Witch*.

sailor

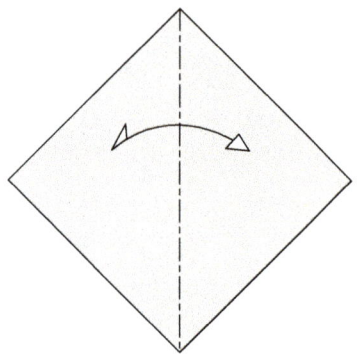

1. Precrease the diagonal in half with a mountain fold.

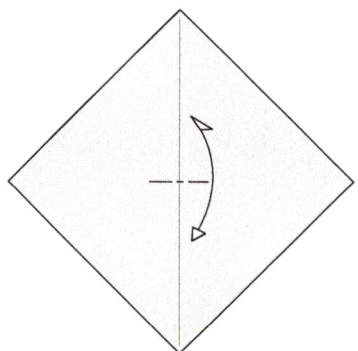

2. Pinch along the center with a mountain fold.

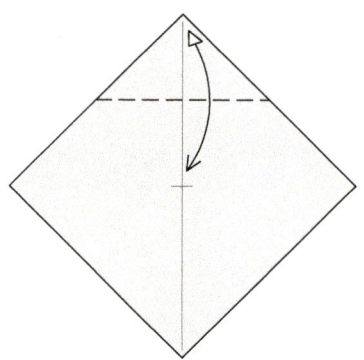

3. Precrease to the center.

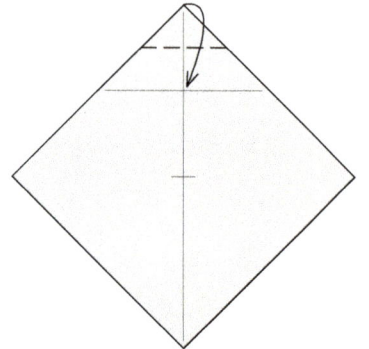

4. Valley fold to the last crease.

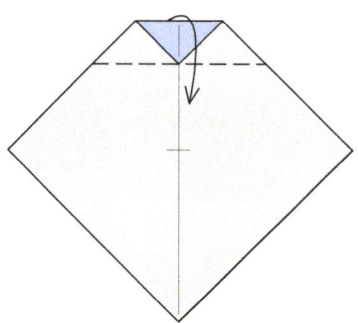

5. Valley fold along the existing crease.

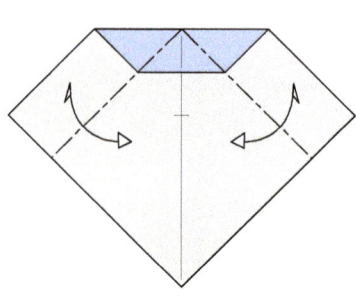

6. Precrease the sides with mountain folds.

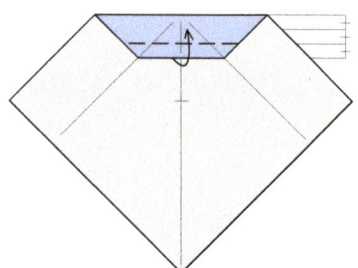

7. Valley fold the edge up at 1/3rd the height.

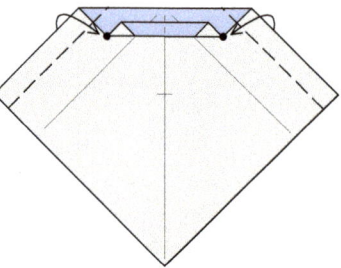

8. Valley fold the sides to meet the dotted corners.

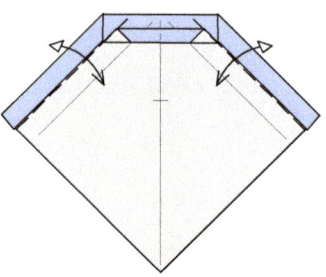

9. Precrease the sides.

sailor

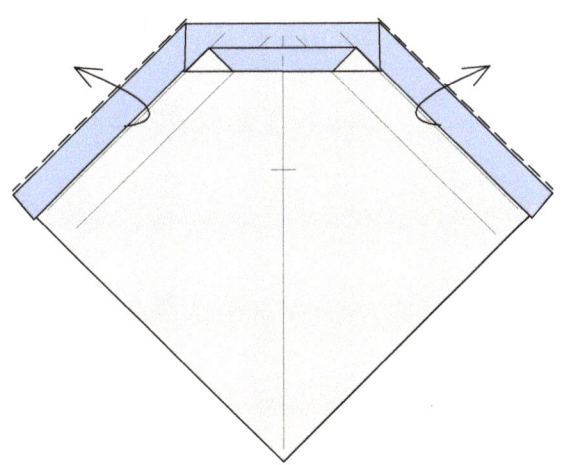

10. Unfold the sides.

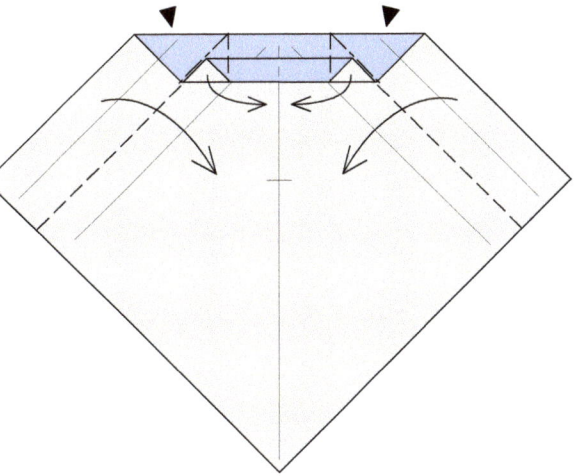

11. Squash fold the sides using the existing creases.

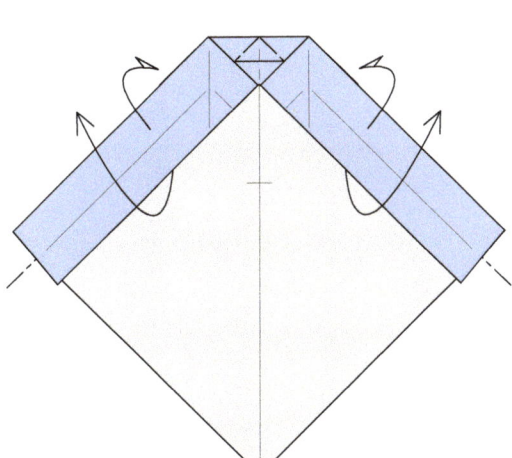

12. Flip the edges behind along the existing creases.

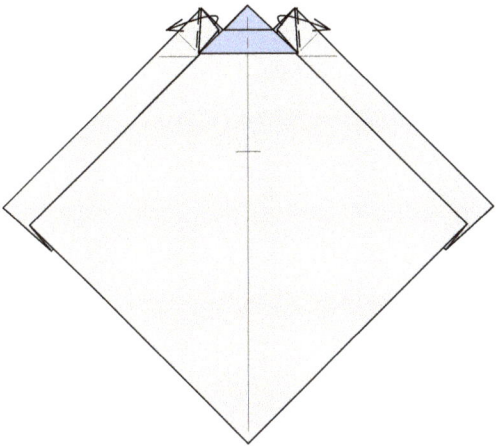

13. Slide out a trapped single layer at each side.

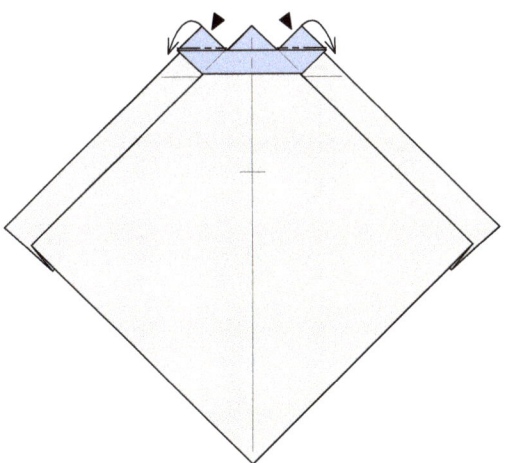

14. Reverse fold the corners.

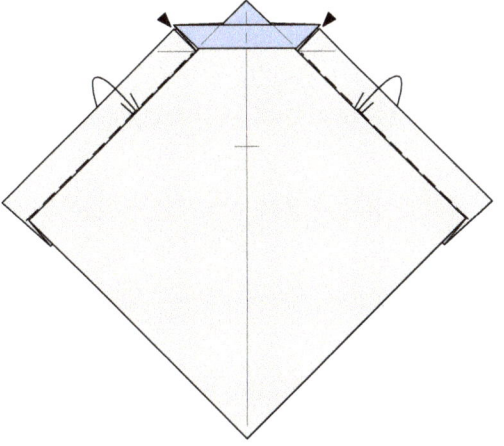

15. Reverse fold the edges into the pockets.

sailor

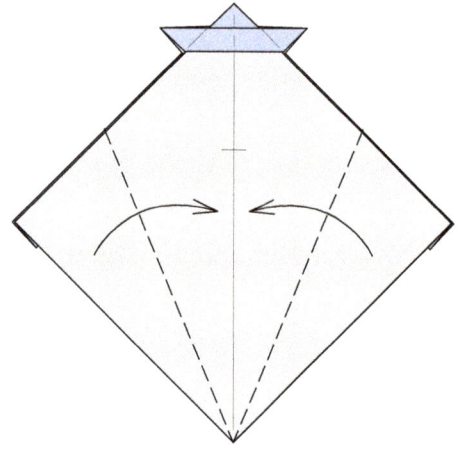

16. Valley fold the sides to the center.

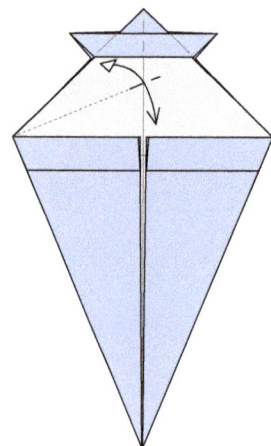

17. Pinch the middle along the indicated angle bisector.

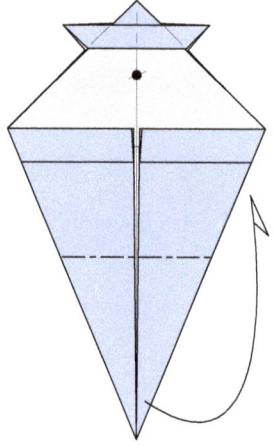

18. Mountain fold the flap to meet the dotted corner.

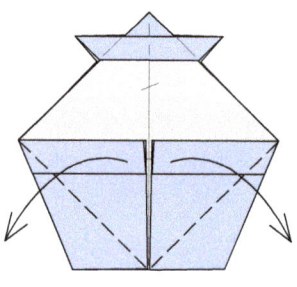

19. Valley fold the top layers outwards.

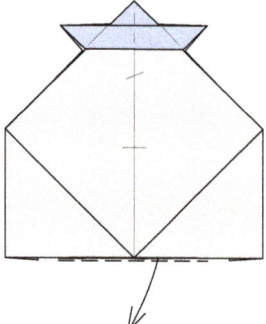

20. Unfold the flap from behind.

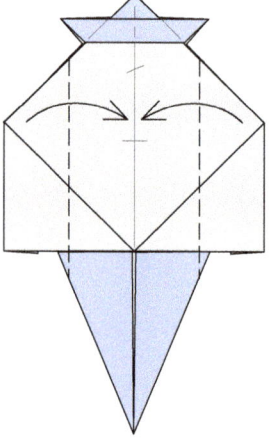

21. Valley fold the sides to the center.

sailor

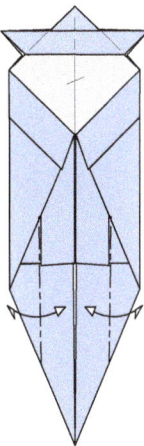

22. Precrease the bottom section with mountain folds, aligning with the folded edges at the middle.

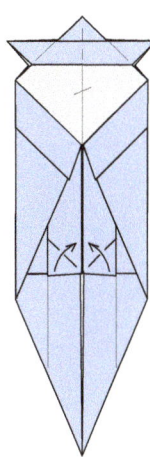

23. Valley fold the corners.

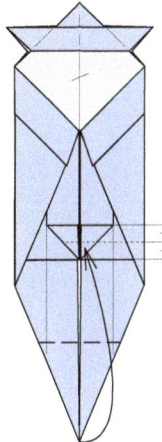

24. Valley fold to the indicated halfway point.

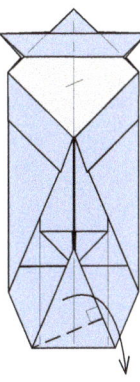

25. Valley fold the flap over, keeping the side edges aligned.

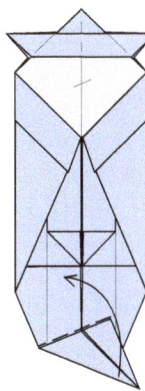

26. Swing the flap back up.

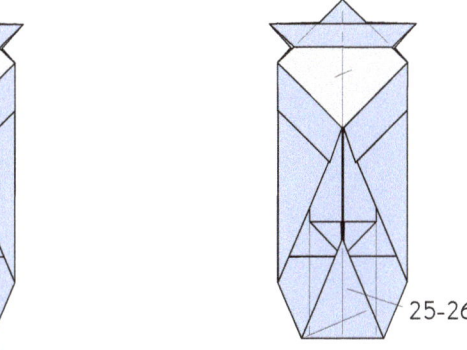

25-26

27. Repeat steps 25-26 in mirror image.

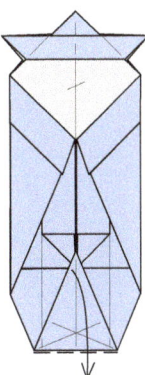

28. Swing the flap down.

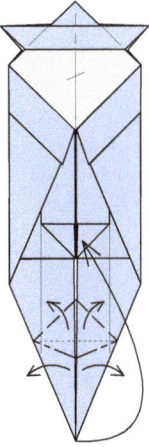

29. Spread apart the top layers while folding the flap up.

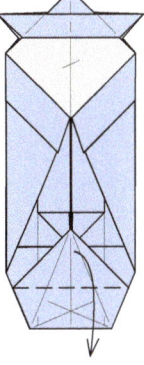

30. Valley fold the top layer down.

sailor

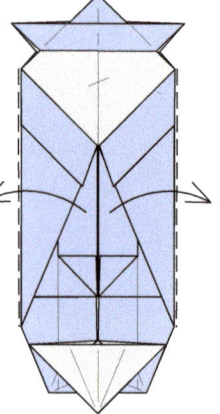

31. Unfold the side flaps.

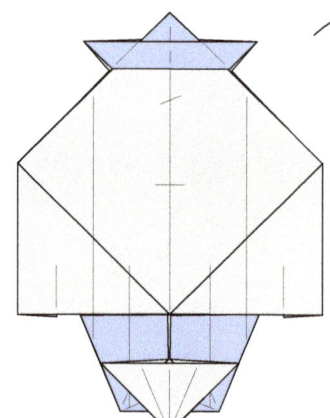

32. Turn over.

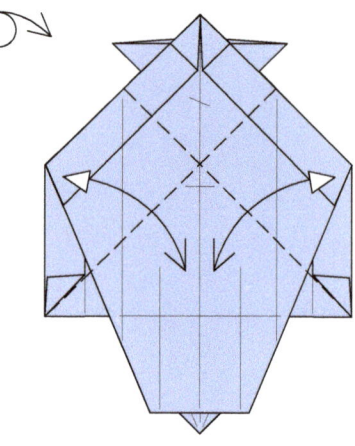

33. Precrease along the angle bisectors.

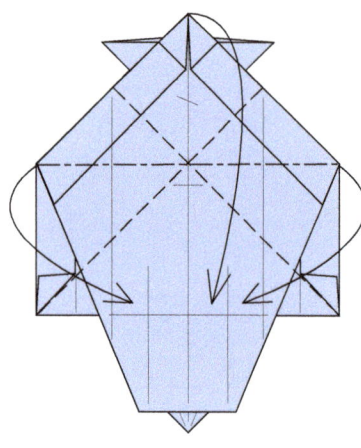

34. Fold the flap down while reverse folding the sides.

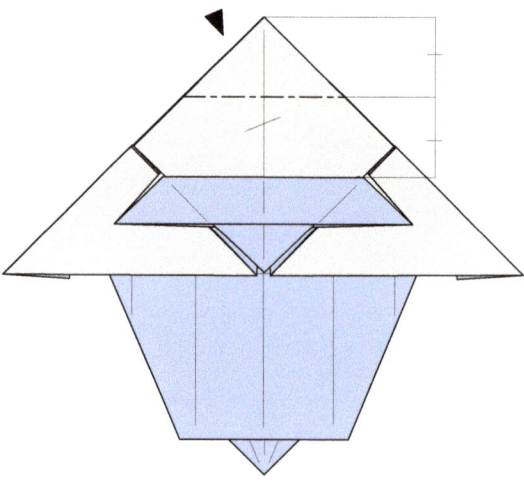

35. Sink the top corner along the indicated halfway division.

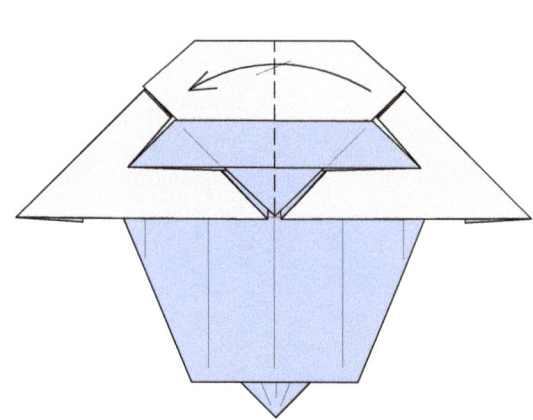

36. Swing over one flap.

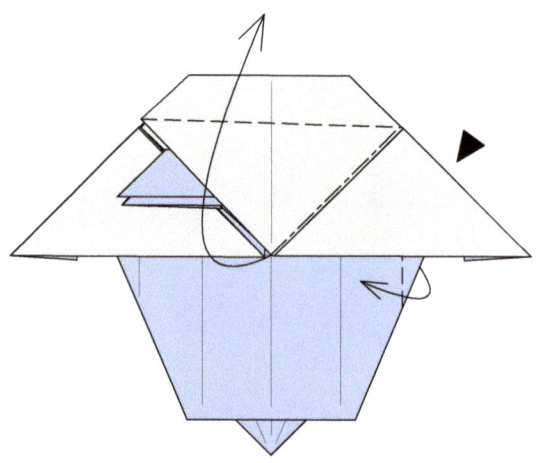

37. Swivel fold the top layer up.

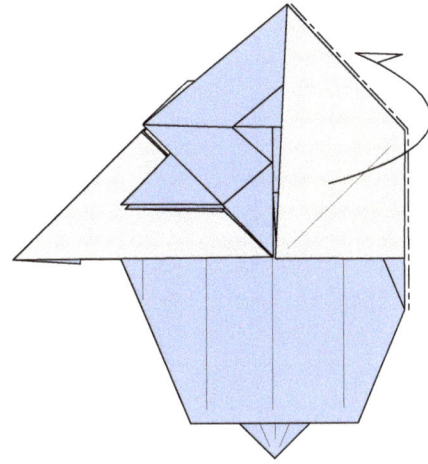

38. Wrap the flap around to the other side.

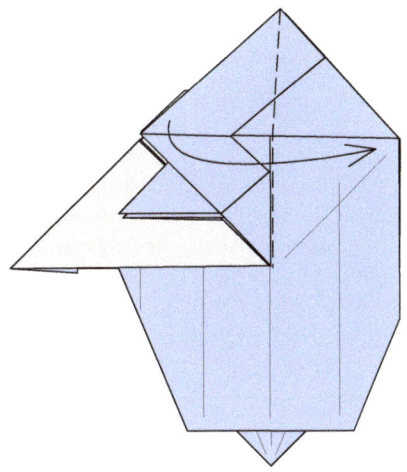

39. Swing one flap over.

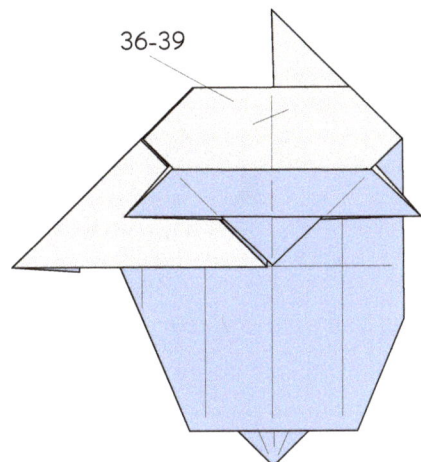

40. Repeat steps 36-39 in mirror image.

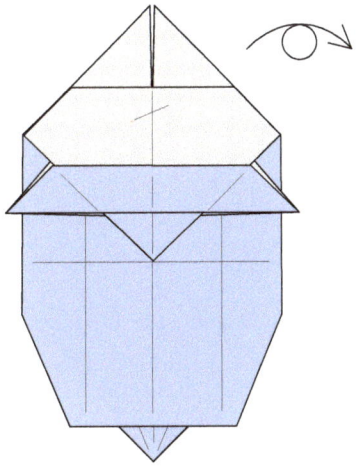

41. Turn over.

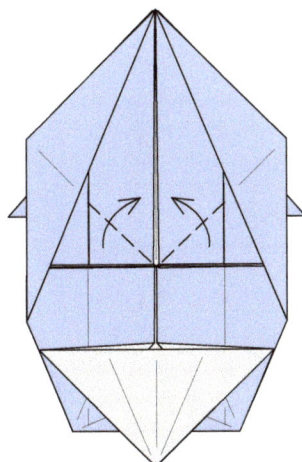

42. Valley fold the corners up (if they came unfolded).

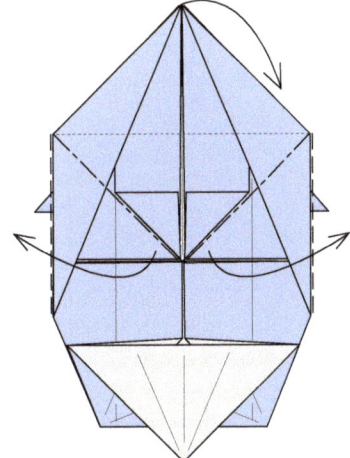

43. Spread apart the side layers while folding the top section down.

sailor

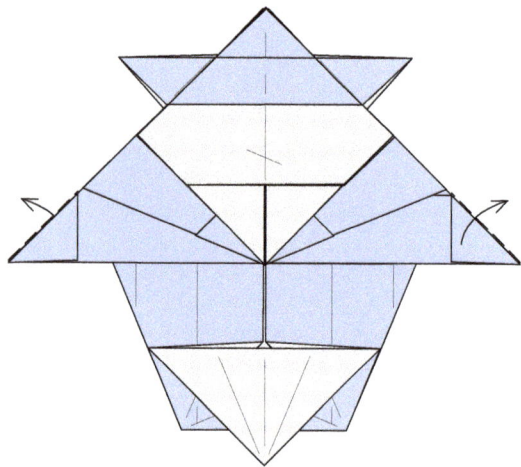

44. Swing the corners back up.

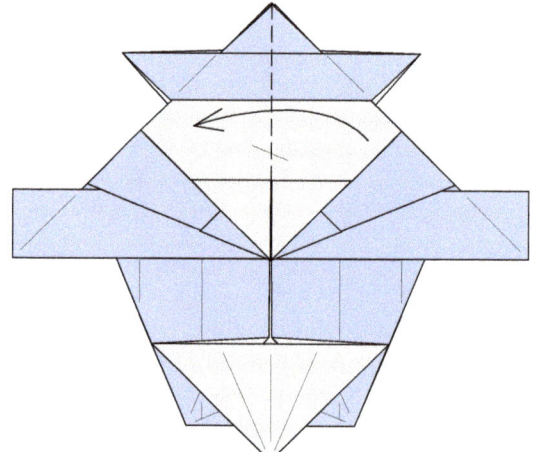

45. Swing over one flap.

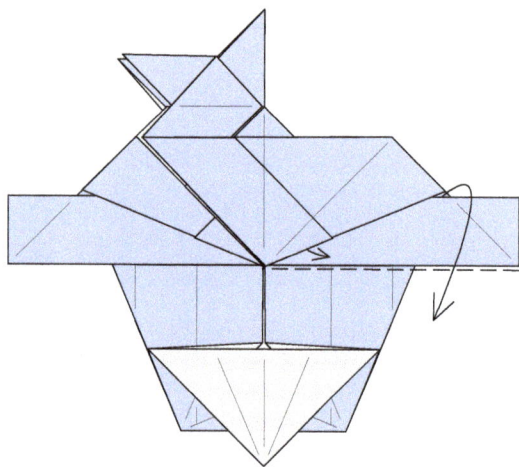

46. Pull out the trapped paper, releasing the top edge. It will not lie flat.

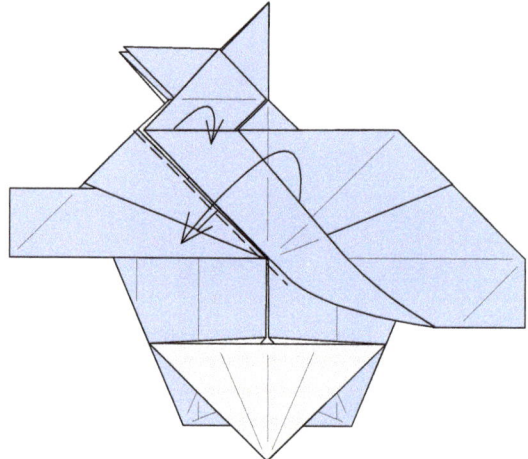

47. Pull out more trapped paper, releasing more of this edge flap.

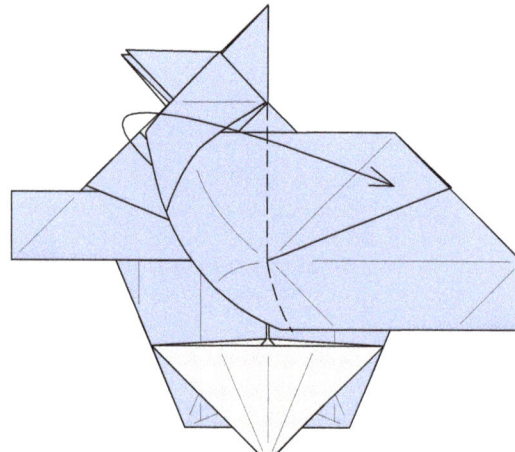

48. Swing the flap over, allowing it to flatten. A small fold should naturally form at the bottom.

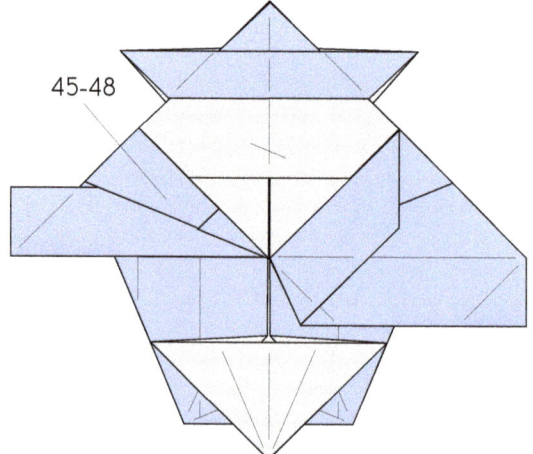

45–48

49. Repeat steps 45–48 in mirror image.

sailor

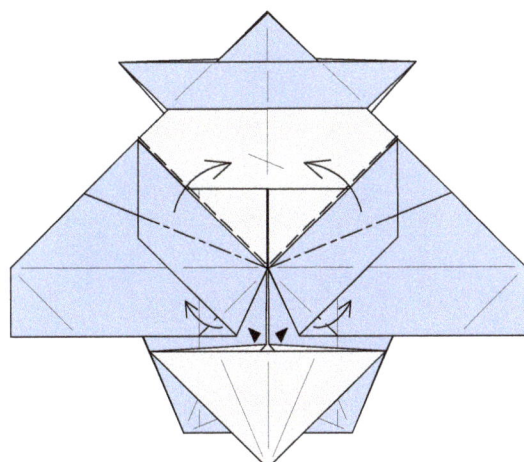

50. Pleat the edges up, while squash folding the bottom corners.

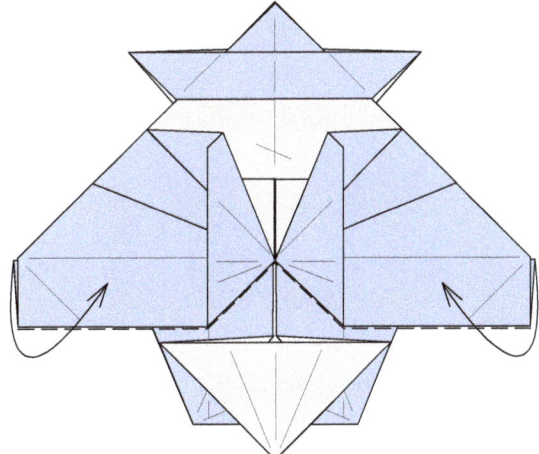

51. Wrap around a single layer at each side.

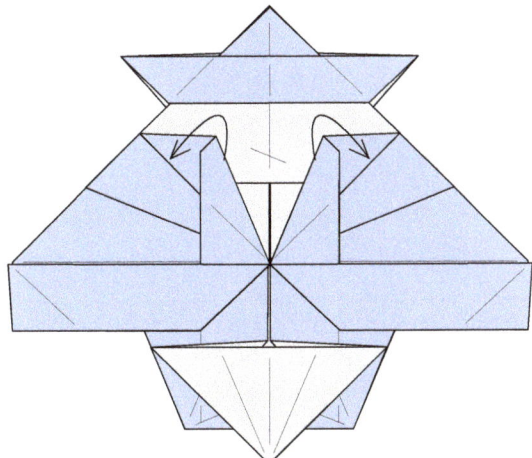

52. Tuck the flaps into the pockets of the flap below.

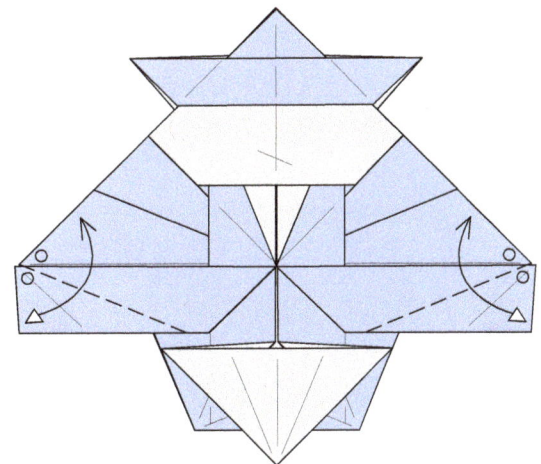

53. Precrease along the indicated angle bisectors.

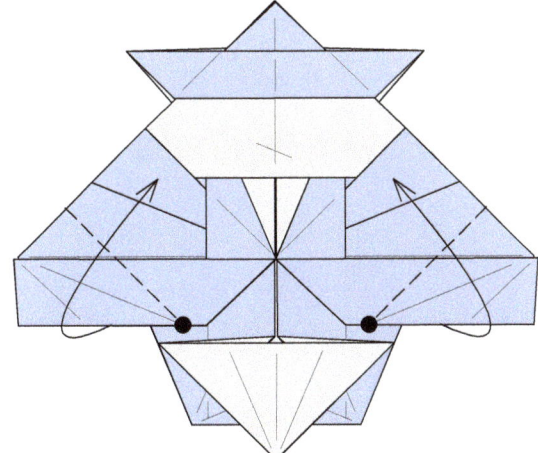

54. Valley fold the sides up starting from the dotted intersections.

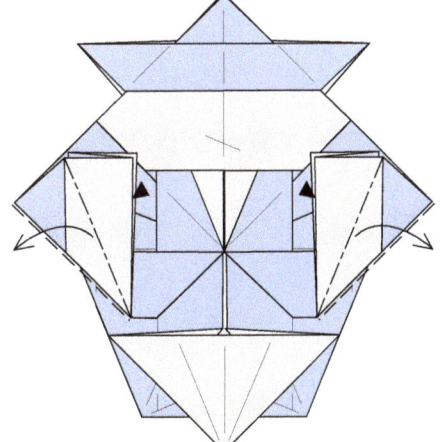

55. Squash fold along the existing creases.

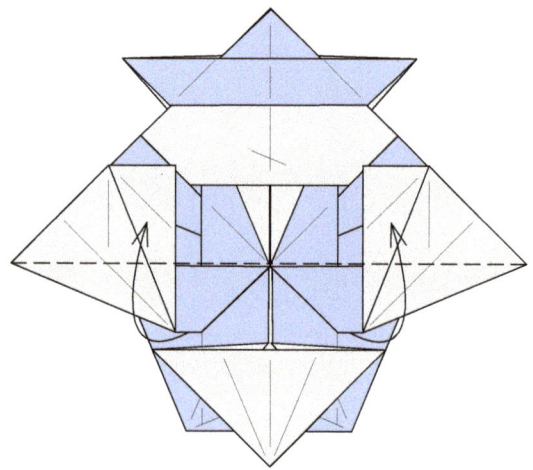

56. Valley fold the edges up.

57. Reverse fold the corners up.

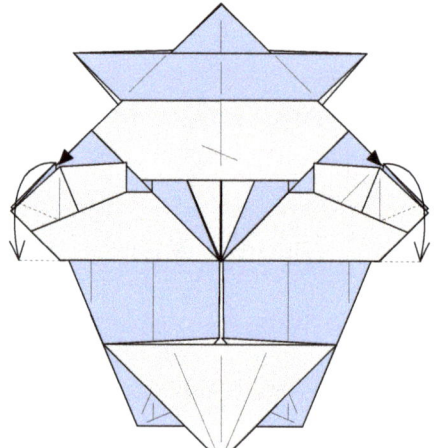

58. Reverse fold the corners down, aligning with the imaginary line.

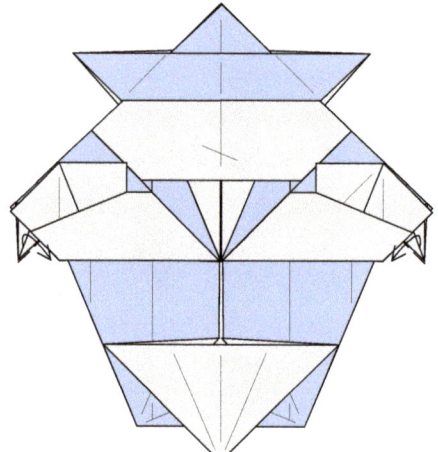

59. Slide the small layers over.

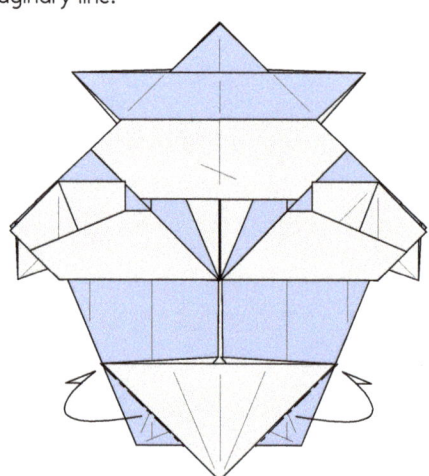

60. Mountain fold the corners behind.

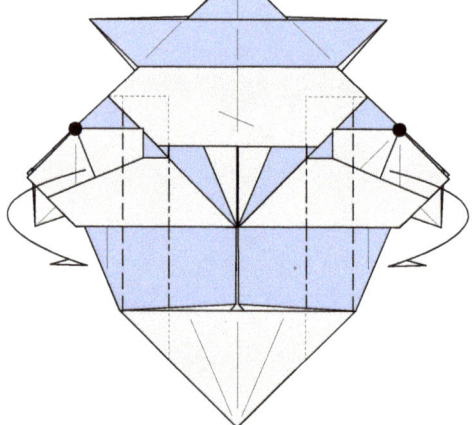

61. Pleat the sides so the dotted corners meet the mountain folds (which are existing creases).

sailor

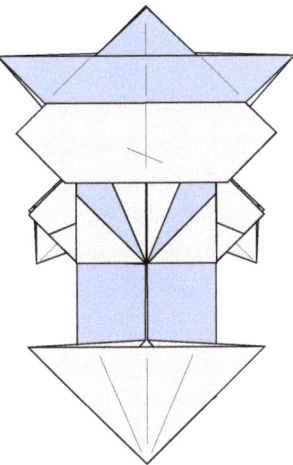

62. Turn over.

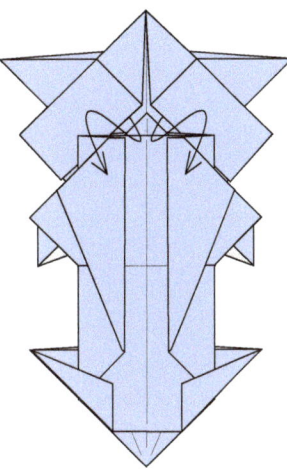

63. Tuck the corners into the pockets.

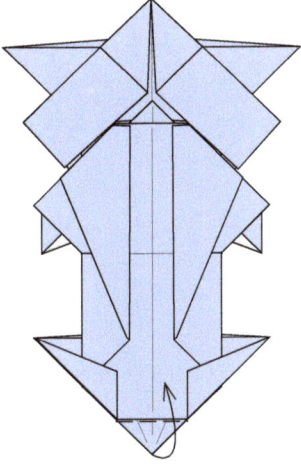

64. Valley fold the corner up.

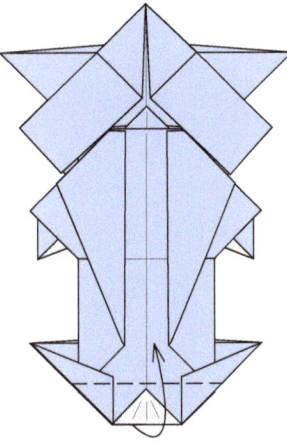

65. Valley fold the bottom section in half.

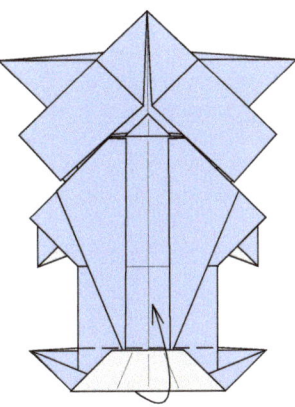

66. Valley fold the bottom section up.

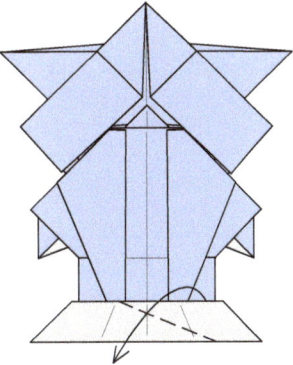

67. Fold the flap down so that the bottom edge lies straight.

109

sailor

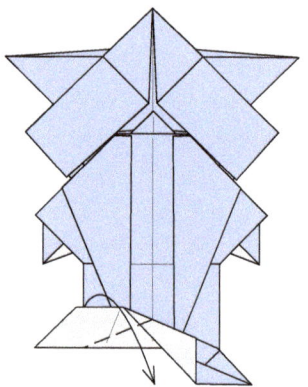

68. Valley fold the other side to match.

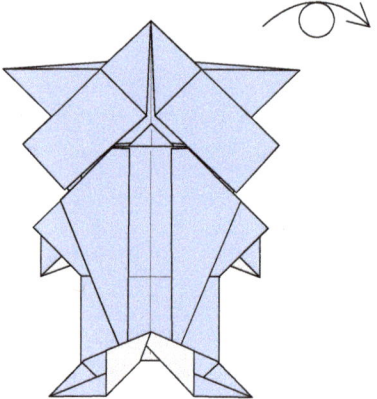

69. Turn over.

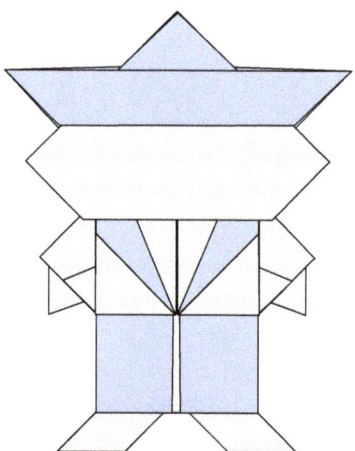

70. Completed *Sailor*.